The
Fiction Writer's Workbook
for Pansters

The Ultimate Character
Building Guide
(*Romance Series Bible*)

Real Love Enterprises

© *2022*

A Real Love Enterprises Publication

ISBN 978-1-958215-11-1

ALL RIGHTS RESERVED.

Series Title: The Fiction Writer's Workbook for Pansters

Title: The Ultimate Character Building Guide - Romance Series Bible

Table of Contents

Introduction

In 2006, when I first put pen to paper and wrote chapter one of my first romance book, I had no clue what I was doing. I thought being an avid romance reader and being one since I was in the 7th grade would help me. It didn't. I had so many questions. I purchased a book, The Complete Idiot's Guide to Writing Erotic Romance, and it gave me the literary rules of the genre, but didn't really tell me how to write my book. Fortunately, I was blessed to find a publisher and editor who thought my talent was worth their time and efforts to mentor me.

I remember the first time I heard the term series bible. I was on book three of my paranormal series, True Mates. This series is set in a small town and has reoccurring characters. I'd described Alex Wolfe's wolf one way in book one and a different way in book three. The line editor caught the error and told me to refer to my series bible. I had no clue what that was. If you're clueless like me, here's the definition from Wikipedia:

> A bible, also known as a show bible or pitch bible, is a reference document used by screenwriters for information on characters, settings, and other elements of a television or film project.

Being the panster that I am, I had no notes, charts, or even spreadsheets as a quick reference guide. If I wanted to know some piece of information, I had to find the book the information was in and read it. I'd seen character development interviews and charts, but who has time for all of that? I wanted to write, not spend twenty-one days prepping to write. That sent me on the great hunt: finding a character building guide or series bible that worked with my creative style of thinking and writing. After several courses, articles, YouTube videos, and workbooks that simply didn't work for me, I decided to create my own.

As a panster, I like to dive right in. That's why I structured the format so a writer can work quickly through the worksheets and spend more time doing what they love best—writing. Unlike my original workbook, this one is created strictly for romance writers and intended to function like a series bible. I know the pain of having to re-read an entire book or series just to ensure I got some miniscule detail correct in my current writing project. I tried using Word documents and Excel spreadsheets, and they worked when I remember to use them. However, I never could get them formatted exactly the way I wanted. Also, it's not always convenient to log into the computer. I wanted the information easily accessible at my fingertips. This workbook is the result.

I hope you find this workbook to be extremely helpful and comprehensive. If nothing else, it should spark your creative juices and get them flowing. I hope you feel the same.

Zena Wynn, Romance Author

No tears in the writer, no tears in the reader. No surprise in the writer, no surprise in the reader.

Robert Frost

Series Tracker

A Quick Glance Guide

Book 1

Working Title:	
Published Title:	
Series Title:	
Point of View:	☐ 1st Person (single) ☐ 1st Person Alternate ☐ 3rd Person
Verb Tense:	☐ Present ☐ Past ☐ Alternate
Romance Subgenres:	☐ Contemporary ☐ Sports ☐ RomCom ☐ African-American ☐ Interracial/Multicultural ☐ Erotic ☐ BDSM ☐ LGBTQ ☐ Paranormal ☐ Regency ☐ Inspirational ☐ Science Fiction ☐ Suspense/ Mystery ☐ Time Travel ☐ Mature (40+) ☐ Urban /Street ☐ Urban/Fantasy ☐ Western/Cowboy ☐ Young Adult/NA
Tropes:	☐ Love Triangle ☐ Billionaire ☐ Friends to Lovers ☐ Forced Proximity ☐ Secret Identity ☐ Second Chance ☐ Soul Mates ☐ Enemies to Lovers ☐ Bully ☐ Fake Relationship ☐ Forbidden Love ☐ Amnesia ☐ Holiday ☐ Military ☐ Roommates ☐ Workplace ☐ Single Parent ☐ Best friend's Brother/Sister ☐ Celebrity/Bodyguard ☐ Marriage of Convenience ☐ Pregnancy (Accidental/Secret Baby/Suddenly Parents ☐ Wedding (Runaway Brides, Best Men, Wedding Planners)
Time Period:	☐ Present Day ☐ Past ☐ Future ☐ Alternate Reality ☐ Time Travel: Future/Past
Romantic Pairing:	☐ Male/Female ☐ Male/Male ☐ Female/Female ☐ Reverse Harem ☐ LGBTQ ☐ MFM ☐ MMF
Format:	☐ Ebook ☐ Print ☐ Audiobook ☐ Reading Apps

Book 1 (continued)

Ebook Publication Date:		Print Publication Date:	
Audiobook Publication Date:		Reading App Publication Date:	
ISBN (ebook)		ISBN (print)	
ISBN (audiobook)		ASIN (ebook)	
ASIN (print)		ASIN (audiobook)	

Blurb:	

Editor:		Final Page Count:	
Publisher:		Total # Episodes:	
Cover Artist:		Narrator:	

DISTRIBUTORS / AGGREGATORS		
☐ Apple Books	☐ Amazon	☐ Barnes and Noble
☐ Draft2Digital	☐ Google	☐ Kobo
☐ Scribd	☐ Ingram Spark	☐ Smashwords

METADATA KEYWORDS

MARKETING STRATEGY	
Short Blurb:	
Tagline:	
Social Media Hashtags	
Social Media Sites:	☐ Facebook ☐ Instagram ☐ Twitter ☐ TikTok ☐ Snapchat ☐ Pinterest ☐ Goodreads ☐ YouTube
Promotion Budget	
Publishing Tasks:	☐ Update Website ☐ Newsletter ☐ Blog ☐ Promo Sites ☐ Schedule Interviews ☐ BookBub ☐ Beta readers ☐ ARC copies ☐ Takeovers
NOTES:	

Book 1 Characters

Character Name	Character Type	Chapter/Scene/ Page#
	Protagonist	
	Protagonist	
	☐P ☐A ☐S ☐M	
	☐P ☐A ☐S ☐M	
	☐P ☐A ☐S ☐M	
	☐P ☐A ☐S ☐M	
	☐P ☐A ☐S ☐M	
	☐P ☐A ☐S ☐M	
	☐P ☐A ☐S ☐M	
	☐P ☐A ☐S ☐M	
	☐P ☐A ☐S ☐M	
	☐P ☐A ☐S ☐M	
	☐P ☐A ☐S ☐M	
	☐P ☐A ☐S ☐M	
	☐P ☐A ☐S ☐M	
	☐P ☐A ☐S ☐M	
	☐P ☐A ☐S ☐M	
	☐P ☐A ☐S ☐M	
	☐P ☐A ☐S ☐M	
	☐P ☐A ☐S ☐M	
	☐P ☐A ☐S ☐M	
	☐P ☐A ☐S ☐M	
	☐P ☐A ☐S ☐M	
	☐P ☐A ☐S ☐M	
	☐P ☐A ☐S ☐M	
	☐P ☐A ☐S ☐M	

Book 2

Working Title:	
Published Title:	
Series Title:	
Point of View:	☐ 1st Person (single) ☐ 1st Person Alternate ☐ 3rd Person
Verb Tense:	☐ Present ☐ Past ☐ Alternate
Romance Subgenres:	☐ Contemporary ☐ Sports ☐ RomCom ☐ African-American ☐ Interracial/Multicultural ☐ Erotic ☐ BDSM ☐ LGBTQ ☐ Paranormal ☐ Regency ☐ Inspirational ☐ Science Fiction ☐ Suspense/ Mystery ☐ Time Travel ☐ Mature (40+) ☐ Urban /Street ☐ Urban/Fantasy ☐ Western/Cowboy ☐ Young Adult/NA
Tropes:	☐ Love Triangle ☐ Billionaire ☐ Friends to Lovers ☐ Forced Proximity ☐ Secret Identity ☐ Second Chance ☐ Soul Mates ☐ Enemies to Lovers ☐ Bully ☐ Fake Relationship ☐ Forbidden Love ☐ Amnesia ☐ Holiday ☐ Military ☐ Roommates ☐ Workplace ☐ Single Parent ☐ Best friend's Brother/Sister ☐ Celebrity/Bodyguard ☐ Marriage of Convenience ☐ Pregnancy (Accidental/Secret Baby/Suddenly Parents) ☐ Wedding (Runaway Brides, Best Men, Wedding Planners)
Time Period:	☐ Present Day ☐ Past ☐ Future ☐ Alternate Reality ☐ Time Travel: Future/Past
Romantic Pairing:	☐ Male/Female ☐ Male/Male ☐ Female/Female ☐ Reverse Harem ☐ LGBTQ ☐ MFM ☐ MMF
Format:	☐ Ebook ☐ Print ☐ Audiobook ☐ Reading Apps

Book 2 (continued)

Ebook Publication Date:		Print Publication Date:	
Audiobook Publication Date:		Reading App Publication Date:	
ISBN (ebook)		ISBN (print)	
ISBN (audiobook)		ASIN (ebook)	
ASIN (print)		ASIN (audiobook)	
Blurb:			
Editor:		Final Page Count:	
Publisher:		Total # Episodes:	
Cover Artist:		Narrator:	

DISTRIBUTORS

☐ Apple Books	☐ Amazon	☐ Barnes and Noble
☐ Draft2Digital	☐ Google	☐ Kobo
☐ Scribd	☐ Ingram Spark	☐ Smashwords

META DATA KEYWORDS

MARKETING STRATEGY

Short Blurb:	
Tagline:	
Social Media Hashtags	
Social Media Sites:	☐ Facebook ☐ Instagram ☐ Twitter ☐ TikTok ☐ Snapchat ☐ Pinterest ☐ Goodreads ☐ YouTube
Promotion Budget	
Publishing Tasks:	☐ Update Website ☐ Newsletter ☐ Blog ☐ Promo Sites ☐ Schedule Interviews ☐ BookBub ☐ Beta readers ☐ ARC copies ☐ Takeovers
NOTES:	

Book 2 Characters

Character Name	Character Type	Chapter/Scene/ Page#
	Protagonist	
	Protagonist	
	☐ P ☐ A ☐ S ☐ M	
	☐ P ☐ A ☐ S ☐ M	
	☐ P ☐ A ☐ S ☐ M	
	☐ P ☐ A ☐ S ☐ M	
	☐ P ☐ A ☐ S ☐ M	
	☐ P ☐ A ☐ S ☐ M	
	☐ P ☐ A ☐ S ☐ M	
	☐ P ☐ A ☐ S ☐ M	
	☐ P ☐ A ☐ S ☐ M	
	☐ P ☐ A ☐ S ☐ M	
	☐ P ☐ A ☐ S ☐ M	
	☐ P ☐ A ☐ S ☐ M	
	☐ P ☐ A ☐ S ☐ M	
	☐ P ☐ A ☐ S ☐ M	
	☐ P ☐ A ☐ S ☐ M	
	☐ P ☐ A ☐ S ☐ M	
	☐ P ☐ A ☐ S ☐ M	
	☐ P ☐ A ☐ S ☐ M	
	☐ P ☐ A ☐ S ☐ M	
	☐ P ☐ A ☐ S ☐ M	
	☐ P ☐ A ☐ S ☐ M	
	☐ P ☐ A ☐ S ☐ M	
	☐ P ☐ A ☐ S ☐ M	

Book 3

Working Title:	
Published Title:	
Series Title:	
Point of View:	☐ 1st Person (single) ☐ 1st Person Alternate ☐ 3rd Person
Verb Tense:	☐ Present ☐ Past ☐ Alternate
Romance Subgenres:	☐ Contemporary ☐ Sports ☐ RomCom ☐ African-American ☐ Interracial/Multicultural ☐ Erotic ☐ BDSM ☐ LGBTQ ☐ Paranormal ☐ Regency ☐ Inspirational ☐ Science Fiction ☐ Suspense/ Mystery ☐ Time Travel ☐ Mature (40+) ☐ Urban /Street ☐ Urban/Fantasy ☐ Western/Cowboy ☐ Young Adult/NA
Tropes:	☐ Love Triangle ☐ Billionaire ☐ Friends to Lovers ☐ Forced Proximity ☐ Secret Identity ☐ Second Chance ☐ Soul Mates ☐ Enemies to Lovers ☐ Bully ☐ Fake Relationship ☐ Forbidden Love ☐ Amnesia ☐ Holiday ☐ Military ☐ Roommates ☐ Workplace ☐ Single Parent ☐ Best friend's Brother/Sister ☐ Celebrity/Bodyguard ☐ Marriage of Convenience ☐ Pregnancy (Accidental/Secret Baby/Suddenly Parents ☐ Wedding (Runaway Brides, Best Men, Wedding Planners)
Time Period:	☐ Present Day ☐ Past ☐ Future ☐ Alternate Reality ☐ Time Travel: Future/Past
Romantic Pairing:	☐ Male/Female ☐ Male/Male ☐ Female/Female ☐ Reverse Harem ☐ LGBTQ ☐ MFM ☐ MMF
Format:	☐ Ebook ☐ Print ☐ Audiobook ☐ Reading Apps

Ebook Publication Date:		Print Publication Date:	
Audiobook Publication Date:		Reading App Publication Date:	
ISBN (ebook)		ISBN (print)	
ISBN (audiobook)		ASIN (ebook)	
ASIN (print)		ASIN (audiobook)	
Blurb:			
Editor:		Final Page Count:	
Publisher:		Total # Episodes:	
Cover Artist:		Narrator:	

DISTRIBUTORS

☐ Apple Books	☐ Amazon	☐ Barnes and Noble
☐ Draft2Digital	☐ Google	☐ Kobo
☐ Scribd	☐ Ingram Spark	☐ Smashwords

KEYWORDS

MARKETING STRATEGY

Short Blurb:	
Tagline:	
Social Media Hashtags:	
Social Media Sites:	☐ Facebook ☐ Instagram ☐ Twitter ☐ TikTok ☐ Snapchat ☐ Pinterest ☐ Goodreads ☐ YouTube
Promotion Budget	
Publishing Tasks:	☐ Update Website ☐ Newsletter ☐ Blog ☐ Promo Sites ☐ Schedule Interviews ☐ BookBub ☐ Beta readers ☐ ARC copies ☐ Takeovers

NOTES:

Book 3 Characters

Character Name	Character Type	Chapter/Scene/Page#
	Protagonist	
	Protagonist	
	☐P ☐A ☐S ☐M	
	☐P ☐A ☐S ☐M	
	☐P ☐A ☐S ☐M	
	☐P ☐A ☐S ☐M	
	☐P ☐A ☐S ☐M	
	☐P ☐A ☐S ☐M	
	☐P ☐A ☐S ☐M	
	☐P ☐A ☐S ☐M	
	☐P ☐A ☐S ☐M	
	☐P ☐A ☐S ☐M	
	☐P ☐A ☐S ☐M	
	☐P ☐A ☐S ☐M	
	☐P ☐A ☐S ☐M	
	☐P ☐A ☐S ☐M	
	☐P ☐A ☐S ☐M	
	☐P ☐A ☐S ☐M	
	☐P ☐A ☐S ☐M	
	☐P ☐A ☐S ☐M	
	☐P ☐A ☐S ☐M	
	☐P ☐A ☐S ☐M	
	☐P ☐A ☐S ☐M	
	☐P ☐A ☐S ☐M	

A good movie makes the audience feel like they've journeyed with the characters.

Rich Moore

Characters

A character is any person, animal, or figure represented in a literary work.

Section 1:

Protagonists

Protagonists are the main characters upon which your story is built. To fully engage readers, they must feel as though they know them and become invested in their outcome. In romances, the reader wants to see themselves in the heroine and fall in love with the hero. They want to root for the couple to overcome all odds and achieve their happily ever after ending. This all begins with building fully fleshed out, relatable characters.

Protagonist # 1

First Name:		Last Name:	
Name Meaning:		Name Meaning:	
Birth Month:		Age:	

Sexual Identity: ☐ Male ☐ Female ☐ Transgender ☐ Nonbinary

Race: ☐ White ☐ Black ☐ Native American ☐ Asian ☐ Pacific Islander ☐ Hispanic ☐ Mixed Race

Ethnicity/ Ancestry:		Religion:	

Species: ☐ Human ☐ Alien ☐ Vampire ☐ Shifter ☐ Fae ☐ Ghost ☐ Mythological god ☐ Witch/Mage ☐ Demon ☐ Mermaid ☐ Djinn ☐ Angels ☐ Gargoyles ☐ Cyborg

Education: ☐ PhD ☐ Masters ☐ 4-year ☐ 2-year ☐ Technical School ☐ High School Graduate ☐ GED ☐ HS Drop Out

Languages: ☐ English ☐ Mandarin ☐ Hindi ☐ Spanish ☐ French ☐ Arabic ☐ Russian ☐ ASL

Dialect/Accent:

Marital Status: ☐ Single ☐ Married ☐ Widowed ☐ Divorced ☐ Separated ☐ Polygamist

Skills/ Hobbies:		Pets:	

Socioeconomic Status: ☐ Top 2% ☐ Wealthy ☐ Poor ☐ Upper Middle Class ☐ Middle Class ☐ Lower Class

Occupation		Employer	

Military: ☐ Never Served ☐ Active Duty ☐ Retired ☐ Honorable Discharge ☐ Dishonorable Discharge

Branch Served:		Years Served:	

Rank/Title:

Criminal Record: ☐ None ☐ Misdemeanor ☐ Felony

Notes, Research, Links

DESCRIPTION			
Height:		**Weight:**	
Eye Color:		**Hair Color:**	
Complexion / Skin Tone:			
Hair Texture:		**Hair Length:**	

Shape of Face: ☐ Square ☐ Oval ☐ Rectangle/Oblong ☐ Round
☐ Diamond ☐ Triangle

Distinguishing Marks:		**Tattoos:**	

Vision: ☐ 20/20 ☐ Glasses ☐ Contacts ☐ Blind
☐ Astigmatism ☐ Nearsighted ☐ Farsighted ☐ Cataracts

Physical Limitations:		**Mental Limitations:**	
Medical Conditions:		**Allergies:**	

Body Type: ☐ Ectomorph ☐ Mesomorph ☐ Endomorph

Body Shape (female): ☐ Rectangle/Straight ☐ Apple
☐ Pear/Triangle ☐ Hourglass

Bust Size: ☐ AA ☐ A ☐ B ☐ C ☐ D ☐ DD ☐ E ☐ F ☐ G ☐ Larger

BACKGROUND			
Native Country:		**Native Language:**	
State/ Provence:		**City / Town:**	

Childhood Home: ☐ Single Family ☐ Townhome ☐ Apartment/Condo
☐ Mobile Home ☐ Farm ☐ Ranch
☐ Multiple Residences/Homes ☐ Homeless

Raised by: ☐ Both Parents ☐ Single Parent ☐ Relative
☐ Foster Care ☐ Orphan ☐ Adopted ☐ Non-Relative

Birth Order: ☐ Oldest ☐ Middle ☐ Youngest ☐ Twin

Parent Name:		**Parent Name:**	
Parent Occupation:		**Parent Occupation:**	

Number of Siblings:

Sibling Names:

Notes, Research, Links

PERSONALITY

Personality Type: ☐ Introvert ☐ Extrovert

Demeanor/Temperament:
☐ Friendly ☐ Cheerful ☐ Arrogant/Haughty ☐ Reserved
☐ Down to Earth ☐ Stoic ☐ Self-Absorbed ☐ Brooding
☐ Laidback ☐ Uptight ☐ Excitable ☐ Surly

Character Trait: ☐ Hero ☐ Antihero ☐ Villain
☐ Martyr ☐ Victim

Communication Style: ☐ Nonverbal ☐ Monosyllabic ☐ Normal
☐ Speaks only when spoken to ☐ Gregarious ☐ Sign Language

Phobias:

Quirks:

Unhealthy Habits: ☐ Tobacco ☐ Alcohol ☐ Drugs

Strengths/Weaknesses:

Closely Held Secret:

SEXUALITY

Sexual Partner Preference: ☐ Heterosexual ☐ Homosexual ☐ Bisexual ☐ Asexual
☐ Other:

Sexual Experience: ☐ Virgin ☐ Novice ☐ Experienced

Type of Sex Preferred:
☐ Vanilla/Traditional ☐ BDSM ☐ Kink ☐ Multiples ☐ Swing
☐ Other:

FASHION STYLE

Personal Preference: ☐ Professional ☐ Business Casual ☐ Casual
☐ Athletic Wear ☐ Glam ☐ Minimalist ☐ Edgy

Fit: ☐ Tailored ☐ Figure-Hugging ☐ Skin Tight
☐ Loose ☐ Baggy ☐ Skimpy

RELATIONSHIPS

Family Structure: ☐ Close Knit ☐ Estranged ☐ Absent ☐ Unknown

Favorite Relative:

Closest Friend:

Relationship History:

As a Neighbor: ☐ Reclusive ☐ Friendly (knows their names)
☐ Knows by Sight Only ☐ No neighbors

Notes, Research, Links

Protagonist # 2

First Name:		Last Name:	
Name Meaning:		Name Meaning:	
Birth Month:		Age:	

Sexual Identity: ☐ Male ☐ Female ☐ Transgender ☐ Nonbinary

Race: ☐ White ☐ Black ☐ Native American ☐ Asian
☐ Pacific Islander ☐ Hispanic ☐ Mixed Race

Ethnicity/ Ancestry:		Religion:	

Species: ☐ Human ☐ Alien ☐ Vampire ☐ Shifter ☐ Fae
☐ Ghost ☐ Mythological god ☐ Witch/Mage ☐ Demon
☐ Mermaid ☐ Djinn ☐ Angels ☐ Gargoyles ☐ Cyborg

Education: ☐ PhD ☐ Masters ☐ 4-year ☐ 2-year ☐ Technical School
☐ High School Graduate ☐ GED ☐ HS Drop Out

Languages: ☐ English ☐ Mandarin ☐ Hindi ☐ Spanish
☐ French ☐ Arabic ☐ Russian ☐ ASL

Dialect/Accent:

Marital Status: ☐ Single ☐ Married ☐ Widowed
☐ Divorced ☐ Separated ☐ Polygamist

Skills/ Hobbies:		Pets:	

Socioeconomic Status: ☐ Top 2% ☐ Wealthy ☐ Poor
☐ Upper Middle Class ☐ Middle Class ☐ Lower Class

Occupation		Employer	

Military: ☐ Never Served ☐ Active Duty ☐ Retired
☐ Honorable Discharge ☐ Dishonorable Discharge

Branch Served:		Years Served:	

Rank/Title:

Criminal Record: ☐ None ☐ Misdemeanor ☐ Felony

Notes, Research, Links

DESCRIPTION			
Height:		**Weight:**	
Eye Color:		**Hair Color:**	
Complexion / Skin Tone:			
Hair Texture:		**Hair Length:**	

Shape of Face: ☐ Square ☐ Oval ☐ Rectangle/Oblong ☐ Round ☐ Diamond ☐ Triangle

Distinguishing Marks:		**Tattoos:**	

Vision: ☐ 20/20 ☐ Glasses ☐ Contacts ☐ Blind
☐ Astigmatism ☐ Nearsighted ☐ Farsighted ☐ Cataracts

Physical Limitations:		**Mental Limitations:**	
Medical Conditions:		**Allergies:**	

Body Type: ☐ Ectomorph ☐ Mesomorph ☐ Endomorph

Body Shape (female): ☐ Rectangle/Straight ☐ Apple ☐ Pear/Triangle ☐ Hourglass

Bust Size: ☐ AA ☐ A ☐ B ☐ C ☐ D ☐ DD ☐ E
☐ F ☐ G ☐ Larger

BACKGROUND			
Native Country:		**Native Language:**	
State/ Provence:		**City / Town:**	

Childhood Home: ☐ Single Family ☐ Townhome ☐ Apartment/Condo
☐ Mobile Home ☐ Farm ☐ Ranch
☐ Multiple Residences/Homes ☐ Homeless

Raised by: ☐ Both Parents ☐ Single Parent ☐ Relative
☐ Foster Care ☐ Orphan ☐ Adopted ☐ Non-Relative

Birth Order: ☐ Oldest ☐ Middle ☐ Youngest ☐ Twin

Parent Name:		**Parent Name:**	
Parent Occupation:		**Parent Occupation:**	

Number of Siblings:

Sibling Names:

Notes, Research, Links

PERSONALITY
Personality Type: ☐ Introvert ☐ Extrovert
Demeanor/Temperament: ☐ Friendly ☐ Cheerful ☐ Arrogant/Haughty ☐ Reserved   ☐ Down to Earth ☐ Stoic ☐ Self-Absorbed ☐ Brooding   ☐ Laidback ☐ Uptight ☐ Excitable ☐ Surly
Character Trait: ☐ Hero ☐ Antihero ☐ Villain   ☐ Martyr ☐ Victim
Communication Style: ☐ Nonverbal ☐ Monosyllabic ☐ Normal   ☐ Speaks only when spoken to ☐ Gregarious ☐ Sign Language
Phobias:
Quirks:
Unhealthy Habits: ☐ Tobacco ☐ Alcohol ☐ Drugs
Strengths/Weaknesses:
Closely Held Secret:

SEXUALITY
Sexual Partner Preference: ☐ Heterosexual ☐ Homosexual   ☐ Bisexual ☐ Asexual ☐ Other:
Sexual Experience: ☐ Virgin ☐ Novice ☐ Experienced
Type of Sex Preferred: ☐ Vanilla/Traditional ☐ BDSM ☐ Kink ☐ Multiples ☐ Swing   ☐ Other:

FASHION STYLE
Personal Preference: ☐ Professional ☐ Business Casual ☐ Casual   ☐ Athletic Wear ☐ Glam ☐ Minimalist ☐ Edgy
Fit: ☐ Tailored ☐ Figure-Hugging ☐ Skin Tight   ☐ Loose ☐ Baggy ☐ Skimpy

RELATIONSHIPS
Family Structure: ☐ Close Knit ☐ Estranged ☐ Absent ☐ Unknown
Favorite Relative:
Closest Friend:
Relationship History:
As a Neighbor: ☐ Reclusive ☐ Friendly (knows their names)   ☐ Knows by Sight Only ☐ No neighbors

Notes, Research, Links

Protagonist # 3

First Name:		Last Name:	
Name Meaning:		Name Meaning:	
Birth Month:		Age:	

Sexual Identity: ☐ Male ☐ Female ☐ Transgender ☐ Nonbinary

Race: ☐ White ☐ Black ☐ Native American ☐ Asian
☐ Pacific Islander ☐ Hispanic ☐ Mixed Race

Ethnicity/Ancestry:		Religion:	

Species: ☐ Human ☐ Alien ☐ Vampire ☐ Shifter ☐ Fae
☐ Ghost ☐ Mythological god ☐ Witch/Mage ☐ Demon
☐ Mermaid ☐ Djinn ☐ Angels ☐ Gargoyles ☐ Cyborg

Education: ☐ PhD ☐ Masters ☐ 4-year ☐ 2-year ☐ Technical School
☐ High School Graduate ☐ GED ☐ HS Drop Out

Languages: ☐ English ☐ Mandarin ☐ Hindi ☐ Spanish
☐ French ☐ Arabic ☐ Russian ☐ ASL

Dialect/Accent:

Marital Status: ☐ Single ☐ Married ☐ Widowed
☐ Divorced ☐ Separated ☐ Polygamist

Skills/Hobbies:		Pets:	

Socioeconomic Status: ☐ Top 2% ☐ Wealthy ☐ Poor
☐ Upper Middle Class ☐ Middle Class ☐ Lower Class

Occupation		Employer	

Military: ☐ Never Served ☐ Active Duty ☐ Retired
☐ Honorable Discharge ☐ Dishonorable Discharge

Branch Served:		Years Served:	

Rank/Title:

Criminal Record: ☐ None ☐ Misdemeanor ☐ Felony

Notes, Research, Links

DESCRIPTION	

Height:		**Weight:**	
Eye Color:		**Hair Color:**	

Complexion / Skin Tone:	

Hair Texture:		**Hair Length:**	

Shape of Face: ☐ Square ☐ Oval ☐ Rectangle/Oblong ☐ Round
☐ Diamond ☐ Triangle

Distinguishing Marks:		**Tattoos:**	

Vision: ☐ 20/20 ☐ Glasses ☐ Contacts ☐ Blind
☐ Astigmatism ☐ Nearsighted ☐ Farsighted ☐ Cataracts

Physical Limitations:		**Mental Limitations:**	
Medical Conditions:		**Allergies:**	

Body Type: ☐ Ectomorph ☐ Mesomorph ☐ Endomorph

Body Shape (female): ☐ Rectangle/Straight ☐ Apple
☐ Pear/Triangle ☐ Hourglass

Bust Size: ☐ AA ☐ A ☐ B ☐ C ☐ D ☐ DD ☐ E ☐ F ☐ G ☐ Larger

BACKGROUND	

Native Country:		**Native Language:**	
State/ Provence:		**City / Town:**	

Childhood Home: ☐ Single Family ☐ Townhome ☐ Apartment/Condo
☐ Mobile Home ☐ Farm ☐ Ranch
☐ Multiple Residences/Homes ☐ Homeless

Raised by: ☐ Both Parents ☐ Single Parent ☐ Relative
☐ Foster Care ☐ Orphan ☐ Adopted ☐ Non-Relative

Birth Order: ☐ Oldest ☐ Middle ☐ Youngest ☐ Twin

Parent Name:		**Parent Name:**	
Parent Occupation:		**Parent Occupation:**	

Number of Siblings:	
Sibling Names:	

Notes, Research, Links

PERSONALITY		

Personality Type:	☐ Introvert	☐ Extrovert

Demeanor/Temperament:

☐ Friendly	☐ Cheerful	☐ Arrogant/Haughty	☐ Reserved
☐ Down to Earth	☐ Stoic	☐ Self-Absorbed	☐ Brooding
☐ Laidback	☐ Uptight	☐ Excitable	☐ Surly

Character Trait: ☐ Hero ☐ Antihero ☐ Villain
☐ Martyr ☐ Victim

Communication Style: ☐ Nonverbal ☐ Monosyllabic ☐ Normal
☐ Speaks only when spoken to ☐ Gregarious ☐ Sign Language

Phobias:

Quirks:

Unhealthy Habits: ☐ Tobacco ☐ Alcohol ☐ Drugs

Strengths/Weaknesses:	
Closely Held Secret:	

SEXUALITY	

Sexual Partner Preference: ☐ Heterosexual ☐ Homosexual
☐ Bisexual ☐ Asexual ☐ Other:

Sexual Experience:
☐ Virgin ☐ Novice ☐ Experienced

Type of Sex Preferred:
☐ Vanilla/Traditional ☐ BDSM ☐ Kink ☐ Multiples ☐ Swing
☐ Other:

FASHION STYLE	

Personal Preference: ☐ Professional ☐ Business Casual ☐ Casual
☐ Athletic Wear ☐ Glam ☐ Minimalist ☐ Edgy

Fit: ☐ Tailored ☐ Figure-Hugging ☐ Skin Tight
☐ Loose ☐ Baggy ☐ Skimpy

RELATIONSHIPS	

Family Structure: ☐ Close Knit ☐ Estranged ☐ Absent ☐ Unknown

Favorite Relative:	
Closest Friend:	
Relationship History:	

As a Neighbor: ☐ Reclusive ☐ Friendly (knows their names)
☐ Knows by Sight Only ☐ No neighbors

Notes, Research, Links

Protagonist # 4

First Name:		Last Name:	
Name Meaning:		Name Meaning:	
Birth Month:		Age:	

Sexual Identity: ☐ Male ☐ Female ☐ Transgender ☐ Nonbinary

Race: ☐ White ☐ Black ☐ Native American ☐ Asian
☐ Pacific Islander ☐ Hispanic ☐ Mixed Race

Ethnicity/ Ancestry:		Religion:	

Species: ☐ Human ☐ Alien ☐ Vampire ☐ Shifter ☐ Fae
☐ Ghost ☐ Mythological god ☐ Witch/Mage ☐ Demon
☐ Mermaid ☐ Djinn ☐ Angels ☐ Gargoyles ☐ Cyborg

Education: ☐ PhD ☐ Masters ☐ 4-year ☐ 2-year ☐ Technical School
☐ High School Graduate ☐ GED ☐ HS Drop Out

Languages: ☐ English ☐ Mandarin ☐ Hindi ☐ Spanish
☐ French ☐ Arabic ☐ Russian ☐ ASL

Dialect/Accent:

Marital Status: ☐ Single ☐ Married ☐ Widowed
☐ Divorced ☐ Separated ☐ Polygamist

Skills/ Hobbies:		Pets:	

Socioeconomic Status: ☐ Top 2% ☐ Wealthy ☐ Poor
☐ Upper Middle Class ☐ Middle Class ☐ Lower Class

Occupation		Employer	

Military: ☐ Never Served ☐ Active Duty ☐ Retired
☐ Honorable Discharge ☐ Dishonorable Discharge

Branch Served:		Years Served:	

Rank/Title:

Criminal Record: ☐ None ☐ Misdemeanor ☐ Felony

Notes, Research, Links

DESCRIPTION

Height:		**Weight:**	
Eye Color:		**Hair Color:**	

Complexion / Skin Tone:

Hair Texture:		**Hair Length:**	

Shape of Face: ☐ Square ☐ Oval ☐ Rectangle/Oblong ☐ Round
☐ Diamond ☐ Triangle

Distinguishing Marks:		**Tattoos:**	

Vision: ☐ 20/20 ☐ Glasses ☐ Contacts ☐ Blind
☐ Astigmatism ☐ Nearsighted ☐ Farsighted ☐ Cataracts

Physical Limitations:		**Mental Limitations:**	
Medical Conditions:		**Allergies:**	

Body Type: ☐ Ectomorph ☐ Mesomorph ☐ Endomorph

Body Shape (female): ☐ Rectangle/Straight ☐ Apple
☐ Pear/Triangle ☐ Hourglass

Bust Size: ☐ AA ☐ A ☐ B ☐ C ☐ D ☐ DD ☐ E ☐ F ☐ G ☐ Larger

BACKGROUND

Native Country:		**Native Language:**	
State/ Provence:		**City / Town:**	

Childhood Home: ☐ Single Family ☐ Townhome ☐ Apartment/Condo
☐ Mobile Home ☐ Farm ☐ Ranch
☐ Multiple Residences/Homes ☐ Homeless

Raised by: ☐ Both Parents ☐ Single Parent ☐ Relative
☐ Foster Care ☐ Orphan ☐ Adopted ☐ Non-Relative

Birth Order: ☐ Oldest ☐ Middle ☐ Youngest ☐ Twin

Parent Name:		**Parent Name:**	
Parent Occupation:		**Parent Occupation:**	

Number of Siblings:

Sibling Names:

Notes, Research, Links

PERSONALITY

Personality Type: ☐ Introvert   ☐ Extrovert

Demeanor/Temperament:

☐ Friendly	☐ Cheerful	☐ Arrogant/Haughty	☐ Reserved
☐ Down to Earth	☐ Stoic	☐ Self-Absorbed	☐ Brooding
☐ Laidback	☐ Uptight	☐ Excitable	☐ Surly

Character Trait: ☐ Hero   ☐ Antihero   ☐ Villain
        ☐ Martyr   ☐ Victim

Communication Style: ☐ Nonverbal   ☐ Monosyllabic   ☐ Normal
     ☐ Speaks only when spoken to   ☐ Gregarious   ☐ Sign Language

Phobias:

Quirks:

Unhealthy Habits: ☐ Tobacco   ☐ Alcohol   ☐ Drugs

Strengths/Weaknesses:

Closely Held Secret:

SEXUALITY

Sexual Partner Preference: ☐ Heterosexual   ☐ Homosexual
     ☐ Bisexual   ☐ Asexual   ☐ Other:

Sexual Experience: ☐ Virgin   ☐ Novice   ☐ Experienced

Type of Sex Preferred:
☐ Vanilla/Traditional   ☐ BDSM   ☐ Kink   ☐ Multiples   ☐ Swing
☐ Other:

FASHION STYLE

Personal Preference: ☐ Professional   ☐ Business Casual   ☐ Casual
     ☐ Athletic Wear   ☐ Glam   ☐ Minimalist   ☐ Edgy

Fit: ☐ Tailored   ☐ Figure-Hugging   ☐ Skin Tight
     ☐ Loose   ☐ Baggy   ☐ Skimpy

RELATIONSHIPS

Family Structure: ☐ Close Knit   ☐ Estranged   ☐ Absent   ☐ Unknown

Favorite Relative:

Closest Friend:

Relationship History:

As a Neighbor: ☐ Reclusive   ☐ Friendly (knows their names)
     ☐ Knows by Sight Only   ☐ No neighbors

Notes, Research, Links

Protagonist # 5

First Name:		Last Name:	
Name Meaning:		Name Meaning:	
Birth Month:		Age:	

Sexual Identity: ☐ Male ☐ Female ☐ Transgender ☐ Nonbinary

Race: ☐ White ☐ Black ☐ Native American ☐ Asian
☐ Pacific Islander ☐ Hispanic ☐ Mixed Race

Ethnicity/ Ancestry:		Religion:	

Species: ☐ Human ☐ Alien ☐ Vampire ☐ Shifter ☐ Fae
☐ Ghost ☐ Mythological god ☐ Witch/Mage ☐ Demon
☐ Mermaid ☐ Djinn ☐ Angels ☐ Gargoyles ☐ Cyborg

Education: ☐ PhD ☐ Masters ☐ 4-year ☐ 2-year ☐ Technical School
☐ High School Graduate ☐ GED ☐ HS Drop Out

Languages: ☐ English ☐ Mandarin ☐ Hindi ☐ Spanish
☐ French ☐ Arabic ☐ Russian ☐ ASL

Dialect/Accent:

Marital Status: ☐ Single ☐ Married ☐ Widowed
☐ Divorced ☐ Separated ☐ Polygamist

Skills/ Hobbies:		Pets:	

Socioeconomic Status: ☐ Top 2% ☐ Wealthy ☐ Poor
☐ Upper Middle Class ☐ Middle Class ☐ Lower Class

Occupation		Employer	

Military: ☐ Never Served ☐ Active Duty ☐ Retired
☐ Honorable Discharge ☐ Dishonorable Discharge

Branch Served:		Years Served:	

Rank/Title:

Criminal Record: ☐ None ☐ Misdemeanor ☐ Felony

Notes, Research, Links

DESCRIPTION			
Height:		**Weight:**	
Eye Color:		**Hair Color:**	
Complexion / Skin Tone:			
Hair Texture:		**Hair Length:**	

Shape of Face: ☐ Square ☐ Oval ☐ Rectangle/Oblong ☐ Round
☐ Diamond ☐ Triangle

Distinguishing Marks:		**Tattoos:**	

Vision: ☐ 20/20 ☐ Glasses ☐ Contacts ☐ Blind
☐ Astigmatism ☐ Nearsighted ☐ Farsighted ☐ Cataracts

Physical Limitations:		**Mental Limitations:**	
Medical Conditions:		**Allergies:**	

Body Type: ☐ Ectomorph ☐ Mesomorph ☐ Endomorph

Body Shape (female): ☐ Rectangle/Straight ☐ Apple
☐ Pear/Triangle ☐ Hourglass

Bust Size: ☐ AA ☐ A ☐ B ☐ C ☐ D ☐ DD ☐ E ☐ F ☐ G ☐ Larger

BACKGROUND			
Native Country:		**Native Language:**	
State/ Provence:		**City / Town:**	

Childhood Home: ☐ Single Family ☐ Townhome ☐ Apartment/Condo
☐ Mobile Home ☐ Farm ☐ Ranch
☐ Multiple Residences/Homes ☐ Homeless

Raised by: ☐ Both Parents ☐ Single Parent ☐ Relative
☐ Foster Care ☐ Orphan ☐ Adopted ☐ Non-Relative

Birth Order: ☐ Oldest ☐ Middle ☐ Youngest ☐ Twin

Parent Name:		**Parent Name:**	
Parent Occupation:		**Parent Occupation:**	

Number of Siblings:

Sibling Names:

Notes, Research, Links

PERSONALITY

Personality Type: ☐ Introvert ☐ Extrovert

Demeanor/Temperament:

☐ Friendly ☐ Cheerful ☐ Arrogant/Haughty ☐ Reserved

☐ Down to Earth ☐ Stoic ☐ Self-Absorbed ☐ Brooding

☐ Laidback ☐ Uptight ☐ Excitable ☐ Surly

Character Trait: ☐ Hero ☐ Antihero ☐ Villain

☐ Martyr ☐ Victim

Communication Style: ☐ Nonverbal ☐ Monosyllabic ☐ Normal

☐ Speaks only when spoken to ☐ Gregarious ☐ Sign Language

Phobias:

Quirks:

Unhealthy Habits: ☐ Tobacco ☐ Alcohol ☐ Drugs

Strengths/Weaknesses:	
Closely Held Secret:	

SEXUALITY

Sexual Partner Preference: ☐ Heterosexual ☐ Homosexual

☐ Bisexual ☐ Asexual ☐ Other:

Sexual Experience: ☐ Virgin ☐ Novice ☐ Experienced

Type of Sex Preferred:

☐ Vanilla/Traditional ☐ BDSM ☐ Kink ☐ Multiples ☐ Swing

☐ Other:

FASHION STYLE

Personal Preference: ☐ Professional ☐ Business Casual ☐ Casual

☐ Athletic Wear ☐ Glam ☐ Minimalist ☐ Edgy

Fit: ☐ Tailored ☐ Figure-Hugging ☐ Skin Tight

☐ Loose ☐ Baggy ☐ Skimpy

RELATIONSHIPS

Family Structure:	☐ Close Knit ☐ Estranged ☐ Absent ☐ Unknown
Favorite Relative:	
Closest Friend:	
Relationship History:	
As a Neighbor:	☐ Reclusive ☐ Friendly (knows their names) ☐ Knows by Sight Only ☐ No neighbors

Notes, Research, Links

Protagonist # 6

First Name:		Last Name:	
Name Meaning:		Name Meaning:	
Birth Month:		Age:	

Sexual Identity: ☐Male ☐ Female ☐ Transgender ☐ Nonbinary

Race: ☐White ☐ Black ☐ Native American ☐ Asian
☐ Pacific Islander ☐ Hispanic ☐ Mixed Race

Ethnicity/ Ancestry:		Religion:	

Species: ☐ Human ☐ Alien ☐ Vampire ☐ Shifter ☐ Fae
☐ Ghost ☐ Mythological god ☐ Witch/Mage ☐ Demon
☐ Mermaid ☐ Djinn ☐ Angels ☐ Gargoyles ☐ Cyborg

Education: ☐ PhD ☐ Masters ☐ 4-year ☐ 2-year ☐ Technical School
☐ High School Graduate ☐ GED ☐ HS Drop Out

Languages: ☐ English ☐ Mandarin ☐ Hindi ☐ Spanish
☐ French ☐ Arabic ☐ Russian ☐ ASL

Dialect/Accent:

Marital Status: ☐ Single ☐ Married ☐ Widowed
☐ Divorced ☐ Separated ☐ Polygamist

Skills/ Hobbies:		Pets:	

Socioeconomic Status: ☐ Top 2% ☐ Wealthy ☐ Poor
☐ Upper Middle Class ☐ Middle Class ☐ Lower Class

Occupation		Employer	

Military: ☐ Never Served ☐ Active Duty ☐ Retired
☐ Honorable Discharge ☐ Dishonorable Discharge

Branch Served:		Years Served:	

Rank/Title:

Criminal Record: ☐ None ☐ Misdemeanor ☐ Felony

Notes, Research, Links

DESCRIPTION

Height:		**Weight:**	
Eye Color:		**Hair Color:**	

Complexion / Skin Tone:

Hair Texture:		**Hair Length:**	

Shape of Face: ☐ Square ☐ Oval ☐ Rectangle/Oblong ☐ Round
☐ Diamond ☐ Triangle

Distinguishing Marks:		**Tattoos:**	

Vision: ☐ 20/20 ☐ Glasses ☐ Contacts ☐ Blind
☐ Astigmatism ☐ Nearsighted ☐ Farsighted ☐ Cataracts

Physical Limitations:		**Mental Limitations:**	
Medical Conditions:		**Allergies:**	

Body Type: ☐ Ectomorph ☐ Mesomorph ☐ Endomorph

Body Shape (female): ☐ Rectangle/Straight ☐ Apple
☐ Pear/Triangle ☐ Hourglass

Bust Size: ☐ AA ☐ A ☐ B ☐ C ☐ D ☐ DD ☐ E ☐ F ☐ G ☐ Larger

BACKGROUND

Native Country:		**Native Language:**	
State/ Provence:		**City / Town:**	

Childhood Home: ☐ Single Family ☐ Townhome ☐ Apartment/Condo
☐ Mobile Home ☐ Farm ☐ Ranch
☐ Multiple Residences/Homes ☐ Homeless

Raised by: ☐ Both Parents ☐ Single Parent ☐ Relative
☐ Foster Care ☐ Orphan ☐ Adopted ☐ Non-Relative

Birth Order: ☐ Oldest ☐ Middle ☐ Youngest ☐ Twin

Parent Name:		**Parent Name:**	
Parent Occupation:		**Parent Occupation:**	

Number of Siblings:

Sibling Names:

Notes, Research, Links

PERSONALITY

Personality Type: ☐ Introvert ☐ Extrovert

Demeanor/Temperament:
☐ Friendly ☐ Cheerful ☐ Arrogant/Haughty ☐ Reserved
☐ Down to Earth ☐ Stoic ☐ Self-Absorbed ☐ Brooding
☐ Laidback ☐ Uptight ☐ Excitable ☐ Surly

Character Trait: ☐ Hero ☐ Antihero ☐ Villain
☐ Martyr ☐ Victim

Communication Style: ☐ Nonverbal ☐ Monosyllabic ☐ Normal
☐ Speaks only when spoken to ☐ Gregarious ☐ Sign Language

Phobias:

Quirks:

Unhealthy Habits: ☐ Tobacco ☐ Alcohol ☐ Drugs

Strengths/Weaknesses:

Closely Held Secret:

SEXUALITY

Sexual Partner Preference: ☐ Heterosexual ☐ Homosexual
☐ Bisexual ☐ Asexual ☐ Other:

Sexual Experience: ☐ Virgin ☐ Novice ☐ Experienced

Type of Sex Preferred:
☐ Vanilla/Traditional ☐ BDSM ☐ Kink ☐ Multiples ☐ Swing
☐ Other:

Fashion Style

Personal Preference: ☐ Professional ☐ Business Casual ☐ Casual
☐ Athletic Wear ☐ Glam ☐ Minimalist ☐ Edgy

Fit: ☐ Tailored ☐ Figure-Hugging ☐ Skin Tight
☐ Loose ☐ Baggy ☐ Skimpy

RELATIONSHIPS

Family Structure: ☐ Close Knit ☐ Estranged ☐ Absent ☐ Unknown

Favorite Relative:

Closest Friend:

Relationship History:

As a Neighbor: ☐ Reclusive ☐ Friendly (knows their names)
☐ Knows by Sight Only ☐ No neighbors

Notes, Research, Links

Section 2: Antagonists

Antagonist are characters that oppose the main characters. They add tension and conflict to a plot. Sometimes they're villains. More often, they are people who don't want to see the protagonist achieve their goals because of jealousy or greed. In romances, these characters do everything in their power to keep the couple from obtaining their happily ever after.

Antagonist # 1

First Name:		Last Name:	
Name Meaning:		Age:	

Relationship with Protagonist:
☐ Stranger ☐ Acquaintance ☐ Coworker ☐ Lover ☐ Frenemy
☐ Former Love Interest ☐ Relative ☐ Rival

Sexual Identity: ☐ Male ☐ Female ☐ Transgender ☐ Nonbinary

Race: ☐ White ☐ Black ☐ Native American ☐ Asian
☐ Pacific Islander ☐ Mixed Race ☐ Hispanic:

Ethnicity/Ancestry:

Species: ☐ Human ☐ Alien ☐ Vampire ☐ Shifter ☐ Fae
☐ Mermaid ☐ Witch/Mage ☐ Demon ☐ Angels ☐ Djinn ☐ Mythological god
☐ Gargoyles ☐ Psychic ☐ Cyborg ☐ Ghost ☐ Monster

Education: ☐ PhD ☐ Masters ☐ 4-year ☐ 2-year ☐ Tech Program
☐ High School Graduate ☐ GED ☐ Drop Out

Languages Spoken: ☐ English ☐ Mandarin ☐ Hindi ☐ Spanish
☐ French ☐ Arabic ☐ Russian ☐ Other:

Sexual Partner Preference: ☐ Heterosexual ☐ Homosexual ☐ Bisexual ☐ Asexual

Marital Status: ☐ Single ☐ Married ☐ Widowed ☐ Divorced

Occupation:		Employer:	

Socioeconomic Status: ☐ Top 2% ☐ High Class ☐ Upper Middle Class
☐ Lower Middle Class ☐ Lower Class ☐ Poor/Destitute

Criminal Record: ☐ Never Arrested ☐ Misdemeanor ☐ Felon

DESCRIPTION

Height:		Weight:	
Eye Color:		Hair Color:	
Complexion/ Skin Tone:		Hair Texture:	

Notes, Research, Links

Hair Cut/Length:

Shape of Face: ☐ Square ☐ Oval ☐ Rectangle/Oblong ☐ Round
☐ Diamond ☐ Triangle

Distinguishing Marks:

Tattoos:

Physical Limitations:

Mental Limitations:

Medical Conditions:

Body Type: ☐ Ectomorph ☐ Mesomorph ☐ Endomorph

Body Shape (female): ☐ Rectangle/Straight ☐ Pear/Triangle ☐ Apple ☐ Hourglass

PERSONALITY TRAITS

Demeanor/Temperament: ☐ Reserved ☐ Brooding ☐ Friendly ☐ Cheerful
☐ Arrogant/Haughty ☐ Stoic ☐ Down to Earth ☐ Stoic
☐ Self-Absorbed ☐ Surly ☐ Laidback ☐ Uptight ☐ Excitable

Communication Style: ☐ Nonverbal ☐ Monosyllabic ☐ Articulate
☐ Speaks only when spoken to ☐ Gregarious ☐ Sign Language

Character Type: ☐ Classic Villain ☐ Anti-Villain ☐ The Beast ☐ Bully
☐ Authority Figure ☐ Fanatic ☐ Mastermind ☐ Henchmen ☐ Nemeses
☐ Corrupted ☐ Antagonist ☐ Artificial Intelligence (AI) ☐ Machine

Criminal Type: ☐ Stalker ☐ Arsonist ☐ Rapist ☐ Killer ☐ Thief
☐ Predator ☐ Organized Crime ☐ Kidnapper ☐ Cyber Crime
☐ Extortionist ☐ Human Trafficker ☐ Dirty Cop ☐ Psychopath/Sociopath

Unhealthy Habits: ☐ Tobacco ☐ Alcohol ☐ Drugs ☐ Sex

Phobias / Quirks:

NOTES

Notes, Research, Links

PSYCHOLOGY

Objective:	

Motivation: ☐ Greed ☐ Revenge ☐ Jealousy ☐ Justice ☐ Desire ☐ Power ☐ Other:

Obstacles:

What will defeat them?

Closely Held Secret:

Strengths/Weaknesses:

Notes:

Antagonist # 2

First Name:		Last Name:	
Name Meaning:		Age:	

Relationship with Protagonist:
- ☐ Stranger ☐ Acquaintance ☐ Coworker ☐ Lover ☐ Frenemy
- ☐ Former Love Interest ☐ Relative ☐ Rival

Sexual Identity: ☐Male ☐ Female ☐ Transgender ☐ Nonbinary

Race: ☐White ☐ Black ☐ Native American ☐ Asian
☐ Pacific Islander ☐ Mixed Race ☐ Hispanic:

Ethnicity/Ancestry:

Species: ☐ Human ☐ Alien ☐ Vampire ☐ Shifter ☐ Fae
☐ Mermaid ☐ Witch/Mage ☐ Demon ☐ Angels ☐ Djinn ☐ Mythological god
☐ Gargoyles ☐ Psychic ☐ Cyborg ☐ Ghost ☐ Monster

Education: ☐ PhD ☐ Masters ☐ 4-year ☐ 2-year ☐ Tech Program
☐ High School Graduate ☐ GED ☐ Drop Out

Languages Spoken: ☐ English ☐ Mandarin ☐ Hindi ☐ Spanish
☐ French ☐ Arabic ☐ Russian ☐ Other:

Sexual Partner Preference: ☐ Heterosexual ☐ Homosexual ☐ Bisexual ☐ Asexual

Marital Status: ☐ Single ☐ Married ☐ Widowed ☐ Divorced

Occupation:		Employer:	

Socioeconomic Status: ☐ Top 2% ☐ High Class ☐ Upper Middle Class
☐ Lower Middle Class ☐ Lower Class ☐ Poor/Destitute

Criminal Record: ☐ Never Arrested ☐ Misdemeanor ☐ Felon

DESCRIPTION			
Height:		Weight:	
Eye Color:		Hair Color:	
Complexion/ Skin Tone:		Hair Texture:	

Notes, Research, Links

Hair Cut/Length:

Shape of Face: ☐ Square ☐ Oval ☐ Rectangle/Oblong ☐ Round
☐ Diamond ☐ Triangle

Distinguishing Marks:

Tattoos:

Physical Limitations:

Mental Limitations:

Medical Conditions:

Body Type: ☐ Ectomorph ☐ Mesomorph ☐ Endomorph

Body Shape (female): ☐ Rectangle/Straight ☐ Pear/Triangle ☐ Apple ☐ Hourglass

PERSONALITY TRAITS

Demeanor/Temperament: ☐ Reserved ☐ Brooding ☐ Friendly ☐ Cheerful
☐ Arrogant/Haughty ☐ Stoic ☐ Down to Earth ☐ Stoic
☐ Self-Absorbed ☐ Surly ☐ Laidback ☐ Uptight ☐ Excitable

Communication Style: ☐ Nonverbal ☐ Monosyllabic ☐ Articulate
☐ Speaks only when spoken to ☐ Gregarious ☐ Sign Language

Character Type: ☐ Classic Villain ☐ Anti-Villain ☐ The Beast ☐ Bully
☐ Authority Figure ☐ Fanatic ☐ Mastermind ☐ Henchmen ☐ Nemeses
☐ Corrupted ☐ Antagonist ☐ Artificial Intelligence (AI) ☐ Machine

Criminal Type: ☐ Stalker ☐ Arsonist ☐ Rapist ☐ Killer ☐ Thief
☐ Predator ☐ Organized Crime ☐ Kidnapper ☐ Cyber Crime
☐ Extortionist ☐ Human Trafficker ☐ Dirty Cop ☐ Psychopath/Sociopath

Unhealthy Habits: ☐ Tobacco ☐ Alcohol ☐ Drugs ☐ Sex

Phobias / Quirks:

NOTES

Notes, Research, Links

PSYCHOLOGY

Objective:

Motivation: ☐ Greed ☐ Revenge ☐ Jealousy ☐ Justice ☐ Desire
☐ Power ☐ Other:

Obstacles:

What will defeat them?

Closely Held Secret:

Strengths/Weaknesses:

Notes:

Antagonist # 3

First Name:		Last Name:	
Name Meaning:		Age:	

Relationship with Protagonist:
- ☐ Stranger   ☐ Acquaintance   ☐ Coworker   ☐ Lover   ☐ Frenemy
- ☐ Former Love Interest   ☐ Relative   ☐ Rival

Sexual Identity: ☐ Male   ☐ Female   ☐ Transgender   ☐ Nonbinary

Race: ☐ White   ☐ Black   ☐ Native American   ☐ Asian
☐ Pacific Islander   ☐ Mixed Race   ☐ Hispanic:

Ethnicity/Ancestry:

Species: ☐ Human   ☐ Alien   ☐ Vampire ☐ Shifter   ☐ Fae
☐ Mermaid   ☐ Witch/Mage   ☐ Demon   ☐ Angels   ☐ Djinn   ☐ Mythological god
☐ Gargoyles   ☐ Psychic   ☐ Cyborg   ☐ Ghost   ☐ Monster

Education: ☐ PhD   ☐ Masters   ☐ 4-year   ☐ 2-year   ☐ Tech Program
☐ High School Graduate   ☐ GED   ☐ Drop Out

Languages Spoken: ☐ English   ☐ Mandarin ☐ Hindi   ☐ Spanish
☐ French ☐ Arabic   ☐ Russian   ☐ Other:

Sexual Partner Preference: ☐ Heterosexual ☐ Homosexual ☐ Bisexual   ☐ Asexual

Marital Status: ☐ Single   ☐ Married   ☐ Widowed   ☐ Divorced

Occupation:		Employer:	

Socioeconomic Status: ☐ Top 2%   ☐ High Class   ☐ Upper Middle Class
☐ Lower Middle Class   ☐ Lower Class   ☐ Poor/Destitute

Criminal Record: ☐ Never Arrested   ☐ Misdemeanor   ☐ Felon

DESCRIPTION			
Height:		Weight:	
Eye Color:		Hair Color:	
Complexion/ Skin Tone:		Hair Texture:	

Notes, Research, Links

Hair Cut/Length:

Shape of Face: ☐ Square ☐ Oval ☐ Rectangle/Oblong ☐ Round
☐ Diamond ☐ Triangle

Distinguishing Marks:

Tattoos:

Physical Limitations:

Mental Limitations:

Medical Conditions:

Body Type: ☐ Ectomorph ☐ Mesomorph ☐ Endomorph

Body Shape (female): ☐ Rectangle/Straight ☐ Pear/Triangle ☐ Apple ☐ Hourglass

PERSONALITY TRAITS

Demeanor/Temperament: ☐ Reserved ☐ Brooding ☐ Friendly ☐ Cheerful
☐ Arrogant/Haughty ☐ Stoic ☐ Down to Earth ☐ Stoic
☐ Self-Absorbed ☐ Surly ☐ Laidback ☐ Uptight ☐ Excitable

Communication Style: ☐ Nonverbal ☐ Monosyllabic ☐ Articulate
☐ Speaks only when spoken to ☐ Gregarious ☐ Sign Language

Character Type: ☐ Classic Villain ☐ Anti-Villain ☐ The Beast ☐ Bully
☐ Authority Figure ☐ Fanatic ☐ Mastermind ☐ Henchmen ☐ Nemeses
☐ Corrupted ☐ Antagonist ☐ Artificial Intelligence (AI) ☐ Machine

Criminal Type: ☐ Stalker ☐ Arsonist ☐ Rapist ☐ Killer ☐ Thief
☐ Predator ☐ Organized Crime ☐ Kidnapper ☐ Cyber Crime
☐ Extortionist ☐ Human Trafficker ☐ Dirty Cop ☐ Psychopath/Sociopath

Unhealthy Habits: ☐ Tobacco ☐ Alcohol ☐ Drugs ☐ Sex

Phobias / Quirks:

NOTES

Notes, Research, Links

PSYCHOLOGY

Objective:

Motivation: ☐ Greed   ☐ Revenge   ☐ Jealousy   ☐ Justice   ☐ Desire
☐ Power   ☐ Other:

Obstacles:

What will defeat them?

Closely Held Secret:

Strengths/Weaknesses:

Notes:

Section 3:

Secondary Characters

Secondary characters in series frequently become main characters. Sometimes, secondary characters have subplots of their own. Build them carefully. You want them interesting, but don't make them so strong that they overpower your protagonists.

Support Character # 1

First Name:		Last Name:	
Birth Month:		Age:	

Relationship to Protagonist: ☐ Sibling ☐ Friend ☐ Love Interest
☐ Spouse ☐ Ex-lover ☐ Child ☐ Parent ☐ Relative
☐ Coworker. ☐ Boss/Supervisor ☐ Teacher/Mentor ☐ Employee
☐ Neighbor ☐ Leader ☐ Other:

Sexual Identity: ☐ Male ☐ Female ☐ Transgender ☐ Nonbinary

Race: ☐ White ☐ Black ☐ Native American ☐ Asian
☐ Pacific Islander ☐ Mixed Race ☐ Hispanic:

Ethnicity/Ancestry:		Religion:	

Species: ☐ Human ☐ Vampire ☐ Shifter ☐ Fae ☐ Ghost
☐ Mythological god ☐ Witch/Mage ☐ Demon ☐ Angels ☐ Alien
☐ Mermaid ☐ Djinn ☐ Gargoyles ☐ Cyborg ☐ Monster
☐ AI (Artificial Intelligence)

Education: ☐ PhD ☐ Masters ☐ 4-year ☐ 2-year ☐ Tech Program
☐ High School Graduate ☐ GED ☐ Drop Out

Languages Spoken: ☐ English ☐ Mandarin ☐ Hindi ☐ Spanish
☐ French ☐ Arabic ☐ Russian ☐ ASL

Dialect/Accent:

Marital Status: ☐ Single ☐ Married ☐ Widowed
☐ Divorced ☐ Separated ☐ Polygamist

Occupation:		Employer:	
Skills/Hobbies:		Pets:	

Military: ☐ Never Served ☐ Active Duty ☐ Retired
☐ Honorable Discharge ☐ Dishonorable Discharge

Branch Served:		Rank/ Title:	

Socioeconomic Status: ☐ Top 2% ☐ High Class ☐ Upper Middle Class
☐ Lower Middle Class ☐ Lower Class ☐ Poor/Destitute

Criminal Record: ☐ None ☐ Misdemeanor ☐ Felony

Notes, Research, Links

DESCRIPTION			
Height:		**Weight:**	
Eye Color:		**Hair Color:**	
Complexion / Skin Tone:			
Hair Texture:		**Hair Length:**	

Shape of Face: ☐ Square ☐ Oval ☐ Rectangle/Oblong ☐ Round
☐ Diamond ☐ Triangle

Distinguishing Marks:		**Tattoos:**	

Vision: ☐ 20/20 ☐ Glasses ☐ Contacts ☐ Blind
☐ Astigmatism ☐ Nearsighted ☐ Farsighted ☐ Cataracts

Physical Limitations:		**Mental Limitations:**	
Medical Conditions:		**Allergies:**	

Body Type: ☐ Ectomorph ☐ Mesomorph ☐ Endomorph

Body Shape (female): ☐ Rectangle/Straight ☐ Apple ☐ Pear/Triangle ☐ Hourglass

Bust Size: ☐ AA ☐ A ☐ B ☐ C ☐ D ☐ DD ☐ E ☐ F ☐ G ☐ Larger

BACKGROUND			
Native Country:		**Native Language:**	
State/ Provence:		**City / Town:**	

Childhood Home: ☐ Single Family ☐ Townhome ☐ Apartment/Condo
☐ Mobile Home ☐ Farm ☐ Ranch
☐ Multiple Residences/Homes ☐ Homeless

Raised by: ☐ Both Parents ☐ Single Parent ☐ Relative
☐ Foster Care ☐ Orphan ☐ Adopted ☐ Non-Relative

Birth Order: ☐ Oldest ☐ Middle ☐ Youngest ☐ Twin

Parent Name:		**Parent Name:**	
Parent Occupation:		**Parent Occupation:**	

Number of Siblings:
Sibling Names:

Notes, Research, Links

PERSONALITY

Personality Type: ☐ Introvert ☐ Extrovert

Demeanor/Temperament:
☐ Friendly	☐ Cheerful	☐ Arrogant/Haughty	☐ Reserved
☐ Down to Earth	☐ Stoic	☐ Self-Absorbed	☐ Brooding
☐ Laidback	☐ Uptight	☐ Excitable	☐ Surly

Character Trait: ☐ Hero ☐ Antihero ☐ Villain ☐ Martyr ☐ Victim

Communication Style: ☐ Nonverbal ☐ Monosyllabic ☐ Articulate
☐ Speaks only when spoken to ☐ Gregarious ☐ Sign Language

Phobias:

Quirks:

Unhealthy Habits: ☐ Tobacco ☐ Alcohol ☐ Drugs ☐ Sex

Strengths/Weaknesses:

Closely Held Secret:

SEXUALITY

Sexual Partner Preference: ☐ Heterosexual ☐ Homosexual
☐ Bisexual ☐ Asexual ☐ Other:

Sexual Experience: ☐ Virgin ☐ Novice ☐ Experienced

Type of Sex Preferred: ☐ Vanilla/Traditional ☐ BDSM ☐ Kink ☐ Multiples
☐ Swing ☐ Other:

FASHION STYLE

Personal Preference: ☐ Professional ☐ Business Casual ☐ Casual
☐ Athletic Wear ☐ Glam ☐ Minimalist ☐ Edgy

Fit: ☐ Tailored ☐ Figure-Hugging ☐ Skin Tight
☐ Loose ☐ Baggy ☐ Skimpy

RELATIONSHIPS

Family Structure: ☐ Close Knit ☐ Estranged ☐ Absent ☐ Unknown

Favorite Relative:

Closest Friend:

Relationship History:

As a Neighbor: ☐ Reclusive ☐ Friendly (knows their names)
☐ Knows by Sight Only ☐ No neighbors

NOTES:

Support Character # 2

First Name:		Last Name:	
Birth Month:		**Age:**	

Relationship to Protagonist: ☐ Sibling ☐ Friend ☐ Love Interest
☐ Spouse ☐ Ex-lover ☐ Child ☐ Parent ☐ Relative
☐ Coworker. ☐ Boss/Supervisor ☐ Teacher/Mentor ☐ Employee
☐ Neighbor ☐ Leader ☐ Other:

Sexual Identity: ☐ Male ☐ Female ☐ Transgender ☐ Nonbinary

Race: ☐ White ☐ Black ☐ Native American ☐ Asian
☐ Pacific Islander ☐ Mixed Race ☐ Hispanic:

Ethnicity/ Ancestry:		**Religion:**	

Species: ☐ Human ☐ Vampire ☐ Shifter ☐ Fae ☐ Ghost
☐ Mythological god ☐ Witch/Mage ☐ Demon ☐ Angels ☐ Alien
☐ Mermaid ☐ Djinn ☐ Gargoyles ☐ Cyborg ☐ Monster
☐ AI (Artificial Intelligence)

Education: ☐ PhD ☐ Masters ☐ 4-year ☐ 2-year ☐ Tech Program
☐ High School Graduate ☐ GED ☐ Drop Out

Languages Spoken: ☐ English ☐ Mandarin ☐ Hindi ☐ Spanish
☐ French ☐ Arabic ☐ Russian ☐ ASL

Dialect/Accent:

Marital Status: ☐ Single ☐ Married ☐ Widowed
☐ Divorced ☐ Separated ☐ Polygamist

Occupation:		**Employer:**	
Skills/Hobbies:		**Pets:**	

Military: ☐ Never Served ☐ Active Duty ☐ Retired
☐ Honorable Discharge ☐ Dishonorable Discharge

Branch Served:		**Rank/ Title:**	

Socioeconomic Status: ☐ Top 2% ☐ High Class ☐ Upper Middle Class
☐ Lower Middle Class ☐ Lower Class ☐ Poor/Destitute

Criminal Record: ☐ None ☐ Misdemeanor ☐ Felony

Notes, Research, Links

DESCRIPTION

Height:		**Weight:**	
Eye Color:		**Hair Color:**	

Complexion / Skin Tone:

Hair Texture:		**Hair Length:**	

Shape of Face: ☐ Square ☐ Oval ☐ Rectangle/Oblong ☐ Round
☐ Diamond ☐ Triangle

Distinguishing Marks:		**Tattoos:**	

Vision: ☐ 20/20 ☐ Glasses ☐ Contacts ☐ Blind
☐ Astigmatism ☐ Nearsighted ☐ Farsighted ☐ Cataracts

Physical Limitations:		**Mental Limitations:**	
Medical Conditions:		**Allergies:**	

Body Type: ☐ Ectomorph ☐ Mesomorph ☐ Endomorph

Body Shape (female): ☐ Rectangle/Straight ☐ Apple ☐ Pear/Triangle ☐ Hourglass

Bust Size: ☐ AA ☐ A ☐ B ☐ C ☐ D ☐ DD ☐ E ☐ F ☐ G ☐ Larger

BACKGROUND

Native Country:		**Native Language:**	
State/ Provence:		**City / Town:**	

Childhood Home: ☐ Single Family ☐ Townhome ☐ Apartment/Condo
☐ Mobile Home ☐ Farm ☐ Ranch
☐ Multiple Residences/Homes ☐ Homeless

Raised by: ☐ Both Parents ☐ Single Parent ☐ Relative
☐ Foster Care ☐ Orphan ☐ Adopted ☐ Non-Relative

Birth Order: ☐ Oldest ☐ Middle ☐ Youngest ☐ Twin

Parent Name:		**Parent Name:**	
Parent Occupation:		**Parent Occupation:**	

Number of Siblings:

Sibling Names:

Notes, Research, Links

PERSONALITY			
Personality Type:	☐ Introvert	☐ Extrovert	
Demeanor/Temperament:			
☐ Friendly	☐ Cheerful	☐ Arrogant/Haughty	☐ Reserved
☐ Down to Earth	☐ Stoic	☐ Self-Absorbed	☐ Brooding
☐ Laidback	☐ Uptight	☐ Excitable	☐ Surly

Character Trait: ☐ Hero   ☐ Antihero   ☐ Villain   ☐ Martyr   ☐ Victim

Communication Style: ☐ Nonverbal   ☐ Monosyllabic   ☐ Articulate
☐ Speaks only when spoken to   ☐ Gregarious   ☐ Sign Language

Phobias:

Quirks:

Unhealthy Habits: ☐ Tobacco   ☐ Alcohol   ☐ Drugs   ☐ Sex

Strengths/Weaknesses:

Closely Held Secret:

SEXUALITY

Sexual Partner Preference: ☐ Heterosexual   ☐ Homosexual
☐ Bisexual   ☐ Asexual   ☐ Other:

Sexual Experience: ☐ Virgin   ☐ Novice   ☐ Experienced

Type of Sex Preferred: ☐ Vanilla/Traditional   ☐ BDSM   ☐ Kink   ☐ Multiples
☐ Swing   ☐ Other:

FASHION STYLE

Personal Preference: ☐Professional   ☐Business Casual   ☐ Casual
☐ Athletic Wear   ☐ Glam   ☐ Minimalist   ☐ Edgy

Fit: ☐ Tailored   ☐ Figure-Hugging   ☐ Skin Tight
☐ Loose   ☐ Baggy   ☐ Skimpy

RELATIONSHIPS

Family Structure: ☐ Close Knit   ☐ Estranged   ☐ Absent   ☐ Unknown

Favorite Relative:

Closest Friend:

Relationship History:

As a Neighbor: ☐ Reclusive   ☐ Friendly (knows their names)
☐ Knows by Sight Only   ☐ No neighbors

NOTES:

Support Character # 3

First Name:		Last Name:	
Birth Month:		Age:	

Relationship to Protagonist: ☐ Sibling ☐ Friend ☐ Love Interest
☐ Spouse ☐ Ex-lover ☐ Child ☐ Parent ☐ Relative
☐ Coworker. ☐ Boss/Supervisor ☐ Teacher/Mentor ☐ Employee
☐ Neighbor ☐ Leader ☐ Other:

Sexual Identity: ☐ Male ☐ Female ☐ Transgender ☐ Nonbinary

Race: ☐ White ☐ Black ☐ Native American ☐ Asian
☐ Pacific Islander ☐ Mixed Race ☐ Hispanic:

Ethnicity/ Ancestry:		Religion:	

Species: ☐ Human ☐ Vampire ☐ Shifter ☐ Fae ☐ Ghost
☐ Mythological god ☐ Witch/Mage ☐ Demon ☐ Angels ☐ Alien
☐ Mermaid ☐ Djinn ☐ Gargoyles ☐ Cyborg ☐ Monster
☐ AI (Artificial Intelligence)

Education: ☐ PhD ☐ Masters ☐ 4-year ☐ 2-year ☐ Tech Program
☐ High School Graduate ☐ GED ☐ Drop Out

Languages Spoken: ☐ English ☐ Mandarin ☐ Hindi ☐ Spanish
☐ French ☐ Arabic ☐ Russian ☐ ASL

Dialect/Accent:

Marital Status: ☐ Single ☐ Married ☐ Widowed
☐ Divorced ☐ Separated ☐ Polygamist

Occupation:		Employer:	
Skills/Hobbies:		Pets:	

Military: ☐ Never Served ☐ Active Duty ☐ Retired
☐ Honorable Discharge ☐ Dishonorable Discharge

Branch Served:		Rank/ Title:	

Socioeconomic Status: ☐ Top 2% ☐ High Class ☐ Upper Middle Class
☐ Lower Middle Class ☐ Lower Class ☐ Poor/Destitute

Criminal Record: ☐ None ☐ Misdemeanor ☐ Felony

Notes, Research, Links

DESCRIPTION			
Height:		**Weight:**	
Eye Color:		**Hair Color:**	

Complexion / Skin Tone:

Hair Texture:		**Hair Length:**	

Shape of Face: ☐ Square ☐ Oval ☐ Rectangle/Oblong ☐ Round
☐ Diamond ☐ Triangle

Distinguishing Marks:		**Tattoos:**	

Vision: ☐ 20/20 ☐ Glasses ☐ Contacts ☐ Blind
☐ Astigmatism ☐ Nearsighted ☐ Farsighted ☐ Cataracts

Physical Limitations:		**Mental Limitations:**	
Medical Conditions:		**Allergies:**	

Body Type: ☐ Ectomorph ☐ Mesomorph ☐ Endomorph

Body Shape (female): ☐ Rectangle/Straight ☐ Apple ☐ Pear/Triangle ☐ Hourglass

Bust Size: ☐ AA ☐ A ☐ B ☐ C ☐ D ☐ DD ☐ E ☐ F ☐ G ☐ Larger

BACKGROUND			
Native Country:		**Native Language:**	
State/ Provence:		**City / Town:**	

Childhood Home: ☐ Single Family ☐ Townhome ☐ Apartment/Condo
☐ Mobile Home ☐ Farm ☐ Ranch
☐ Multiple Residences/Homes ☐ Homeless

Raised by: ☐ Both Parents ☐ Single Parent ☐ Relative
☐ Foster Care ☐ Orphan ☐ Adopted ☐ Non-Relative

Birth Order: ☐ Oldest ☐ Middle ☐ Youngest ☐ Twin

Parent Name:		**Parent Name:**	
Parent Occupation:		**Parent Occupation:**	

Number of Siblings:

Sibling Names:

Notes, Research, Links

PERSONALITY	
Personality Type:	☐ Introvert ☐ Extrovert
Demeanor/Temperament:	
☐ Friendly ☐ Cheerful ☐ Arrogant/Haughty ☐ Reserved ☐ Down to Earth ☐ Stoic ☐ Self-Absorbed ☐ Brooding ☐ Laidback ☐ Uptight ☐ Excitable ☐ Surly	
Character Trait: ☐ Hero ☐ Antihero ☐ Villain ☐ Martyr ☐ Victim	
Communication Style: ☐ Nonverbal ☐ Monosyllabic ☐ Articulate ☐ Speaks only when spoken to ☐ Gregarious ☐ Sign Language	
Phobias:	
Quirks:	
Unhealthy Habits: ☐ Tobacco ☐ Alcohol ☐ Drugs ☐ Sex	
Strengths/Weaknesses:	
Closely Held Secret:	

SEXUALITY	
Sexual Partner Preference: ☐ Heterosexual ☐ Homosexual ☐ Bisexual ☐ Asexual ☐ Other:	
Sexual Experience: ☐ Virgin ☐ Novice ☐ Experienced	
Type of Sex Preferred: ☐ Vanilla/Traditional ☐ BDSM ☐ Kink ☐ Multiples ☐ Swing ☐ Other:	

FASHION STYLE	
Personal Preference: ☐Professional ☐Business Casual ☐ Casual ☐ Athletic Wear ☐ Glam ☐ Minimalist ☐ Edgy	
Fit: ☐ Tailored ☐ Figure-Hugging ☐ Skin Tight ☐ Loose ☐ Baggy ☐ Skimpy	

RELATIONSHIPS	
Family Structure:	☐ Close Knit ☐ Estranged ☐ Absent ☐ Unknown
Favorite Relative:	
Closest Friend:	
Relationship History:	
As a Neighbor:	☐ Reclusive ☐ Friendly (knows their names) ☐ Knows by Sight Only ☐ No neighbors
NOTES:	

Support Character # 4

First Name:		Last Name:	
Birth Month:		Age:	

Relationship to Protagonist: ☐ Sibling ☐ Friend ☐ Love Interest
☐ Spouse ☐ Ex-lover ☐ Child ☐ Parent ☐ Relative
☐ Coworker. ☐ Boss/Supervisor ☐ Teacher/Mentor ☐ Employee
☐ Neighbor ☐ Leader ☐ Other:

Sexual Identity: ☐ Male ☐ Female ☐ Transgender ☐ Nonbinary

Race: ☐ White ☐ Black ☐ Native American ☐ Asian
☐ Pacific Islander ☐ Mixed Race ☐ Hispanic:

Ethnicity/ Ancestry:		Religion:	

Species: ☐ Human ☐ Vampire ☐ Shifter ☐ Fae ☐ Ghost
☐ Mythological god ☐ Witch/Mage ☐ Demon ☐ Angels ☐ Alien
☐ Mermaid ☐ Djinn ☐ Gargoyles ☐ Cyborg ☐ Monster
☐ AI (Artificial Intelligence)

Education: ☐ PhD ☐ Masters ☐ 4-year ☐ 2-year ☐ Tech Program
☐ High School Graduate ☐ GED ☐ Drop Out

Languages Spoken: ☐ English ☐ Mandarin ☐ Hindi ☐ Spanish
☐ French ☐ Arabic ☐ Russian ☐ ASL

Dialect/Accent:

Marital Status: ☐ Single ☐ Married ☐ Widowed
☐ Divorced ☐ Separated ☐ Polygamist

Occupation:		Employer:	
Skills/Hobbies:		Pets:	

Military: ☐ Never Served ☐ Active Duty ☐ Retired
☐ Honorable Discharge ☐ Dishonorable Discharge

Branch Served:		Rank/ Title:	

Socioeconomic Status: ☐ Top 2% ☐ High Class ☐ Upper Middle Class
☐ Lower Middle Class ☐ Lower Class ☐ Poor/Destitute

Criminal Record: ☐ None ☐ Misdemeanor ☐ Felony

Notes, Research, Links

DESCRIPTION

Height:		Weight:	
Eye Color:		Hair Color:	

Complexion / Skin Tone:

Hair Texture:		Hair Length:	

Shape of Face: ☐ Square ☐ Oval ☐ Rectangle/Oblong ☐ Round ☐ Diamond ☐ Triangle

Distinguishing Marks:		Tattoos:	

Vision: ☐ 20/20 ☐ Glasses ☐ Contacts ☐ Blind ☐ Astigmatism ☐ Nearsighted ☐ Farsighted ☐ Cataracts

Physical Limitations:		Mental Limitations:	
Medical Conditions:		Allergies:	

Body Type: ☐ Ectomorph ☐ Mesomorph ☐ Endomorph

Body Shape (female): ☐ Rectangle/Straight ☐ Apple ☐ Pear/Triangle ☐ Hourglass

Bust Size: ☐ AA ☐ A ☐ B ☐ C ☐ D ☐ DD ☐ E ☐ F ☐ G ☐ Larger

BACKGROUND

Native Country:		Native Language:	
State/ Provence:		City / Town:	

Childhood Home: ☐ Single Family ☐ Townhome ☐ Apartment/Condo ☐ Mobile Home ☐ Farm ☐ Ranch ☐ Multiple Residences/Homes ☐ Homeless

Raised by: ☐ Both Parents ☐ Single Parent ☐ Relative ☐ Foster Care ☐ Orphan ☐ Adopted ☐ Non-Relative

Birth Order: ☐ Oldest ☐ Middle ☐ Youngest ☐ Twin

Parent Name:		Parent Name:	
Parent Occupation:		Parent Occupation:	

Number of Siblings:

Sibling Names:

Notes, Research, Links

PERSONALITY

Personality Type: ☐ Introvert ☐ Extrovert

Demeanor/Temperament:

☐ Friendly	☐ Cheerful	☐ Arrogant/Haughty	☐ Reserved
☐ Down to Earth	☐ Stoic	☐ Self-Absorbed	☐ Brooding
☐ Laidback	☐ Uptight	☐ Excitable	☐ Surly

Character Trait: ☐ Hero ☐ Antihero ☐ Villain ☐ Martyr ☐ Victim

Communication Style: ☐ Nonverbal ☐ Monosyllabic ☐ Articulate ☐ Speaks only when spoken to ☐ Gregarious ☐ Sign Language

Phobias:

Quirks:

Unhealthy Habits: ☐ Tobacco ☐ Alcohol ☐ Drugs ☐ Sex

Strengths/Weaknesses:

Closely Held Secret:

SEXUALITY

Sexual Partner Preference: ☐ Heterosexual ☐ Homosexual ☐ Bisexual ☐ Asexual ☐ Other:

Sexual Experience: ☐ Virgin ☐ Novice ☐ Experienced

Type of Sex Preferred: ☐ Vanilla/Traditional ☐ BDSM ☐ Kink ☐ Multiples ☐ Swing ☐ Other:

FASHION STYLE

Personal Preference: ☐ Professional ☐ Business Casual ☐ Casual ☐ Athletic Wear ☐ Glam ☐ Minimalist ☐ Edgy

Fit: ☐ Tailored ☐ Figure-Hugging ☐ Skin Tight ☐ Loose ☐ Baggy ☐ Skimpy

RELATIONSHIPS

Family Structure: ☐ Close Knit ☐ Estranged ☐ Absent ☐ Unknown

Favorite Relative:

Closest Friend:

Relationship History:

As a Neighbor: ☐ Reclusive ☐ Friendly (knows their names) ☐ Knows by Sight Only ☐ No neighbors

NOTES:

Support Character # 5

First Name:		Last Name:	
Birth Month:		**Age:**	

Relationship to Protagonist: ☐ Sibling ☐ Friend ☐ Love Interest
☐ Spouse ☐ Ex-lover ☐ Child ☐ Parent ☐ Relative
☐ Coworker. ☐ Boss/Supervisor ☐ Teacher/Mentor ☐ Employee
☐ Neighbor ☐ Leader ☐ Other:

Sexual Identity: ☐ Male ☐ Female ☐ Transgender ☐ Nonbinary

Race: ☐ White ☐ Black ☐ Native American ☐ Asian
☐ Pacific Islander ☐ Mixed Race ☐ Hispanic:

Ethnicity/ Ancestry:		Religion:	

Species: ☐ Human ☐ Vampire ☐ Shifter ☐ Fae ☐ Ghost
☐ Mythological god ☐ Witch/Mage ☐ Demon ☐ Angels ☐ Alien
☐ Mermaid ☐ Djinn ☐ Gargoyles ☐ Cyborg ☐ Monster
☐ AI (Artificial Intelligence)

Education: ☐ PhD ☐ Masters ☐ 4-year ☐ 2-year ☐ Tech Program
☐ High School Graduate ☐ GED ☐ Drop Out

Languages Spoken: ☐ English ☐ Mandarin ☐ Hindi ☐ Spanish
☐ French ☐ Arabic ☐ Russian ☐ ASL

Dialect/Accent:

Marital Status: ☐ Single ☐ Married ☐ Widowed
☐ Divorced ☐ Separated ☐ Polygamist

Occupation:		Employer:	
Skills/Hobbies:		**Pets:**	

Military: ☐ Never Served ☐ Active Duty ☐ Retired
☐ Honorable Discharge ☐ Dishonorable Discharge

Branch Served:		Rank/ Title:	

Socioeconomic Status: ☐ Top 2% ☐ High Class ☐ Upper Middle Class
☐ Lower Middle Class ☐ Lower Class ☐ Poor/Destitute

Criminal Record: ☐ None ☐ Misdemeanor ☐ Felony

Notes, Research, Links

DESCRIPTION			
Height:		**Weight:**	
Eye Color:		**Hair Color:**	
Complexion / Skin Tone:			
Hair Texture:		**Hair Length:**	

Shape of Face: ☐ Square ☐ Oval ☐ Rectangle/Oblong ☐ Round
☐ Diamond ☐ Triangle

Distinguishing Marks:		**Tattoos:**	

Vision: ☐ 20/20 ☐ Glasses ☐ Contacts ☐ Blind
☐ Astigmatism ☐ Nearsighted ☐ Farsighted ☐ Cataracts

Physical Limitations:		**Mental Limitations:**	
Medical Conditions:		**Allergies:**	

Body Type: ☐ Ectomorph ☐ Mesomorph ☐ Endomorph

Body Shape (female): ☐ Rectangle/Straight ☐ Apple ☐ Pear/Triangle ☐ Hourglass

Bust Size: ☐ AA ☐ A ☐ B ☐ C ☐ D ☐ DD ☐ E ☐ F ☐ G ☐ Larger

BACKGROUND			
Native Country:		**Native Language:**	
State/ Provence:		**City / Town:**	

Childhood Home: ☐ Single Family ☐ Townhome ☐ Apartment/Condo
☐ Mobile Home ☐ Farm ☐ Ranch
☐ Multiple Residences/Homes ☐ Homeless

Raised by: ☐ Both Parents ☐ Single Parent ☐ Relative
☐ Foster Care ☐ Orphan ☐ Adopted ☐ Non-Relative

Birth Order: ☐ Oldest ☐ Middle ☐ Youngest ☐ Twin

Parent Name:		**Parent Name:**	
Parent Occupation:		**Parent Occupation:**	
Number of Siblings:			
Sibling Names:			

Notes, Research, Links

PERSONALITY			
Personality Type: ☐ Introvert ☐ Extrovert			
Demeanor/Temperament:			
☐ Friendly	☐ Cheerful	☐ Arrogant/Haughty	☐ Reserved
☐ Down to Earth	☐ Stoic	☐ Self-Absorbed	☐ Brooding
☐ Laidback	☐ Uptight	☐ Excitable	☐ Surly
Character Trait: ☐ Hero ☐ Antihero ☐ Villain ☐ Martyr ☐ Victim			
Communication Style: ☐ Nonverbal ☐ Monosyllabic ☐ Articulate ☐ Speaks only when spoken to ☐ Gregarious ☐ Sign Language			
Phobias:			
Quirks:			
Unhealthy Habits: ☐ Tobacco ☐ Alcohol ☐ Drugs ☐ Sex			
Strengths/Weaknesses:			
Closely Held Secret:			

SEXUALITY	
Sexual Partner Preference: ☐ Heterosexual ☐ Homosexual ☐ Bisexual ☐ Asexual ☐ Other:	
Sexual Experience: ☐ Virgin ☐ Novice ☐ Experienced	
Type of Sex Preferred: ☐ Vanilla/Traditional ☐ BDSM ☐ Kink ☐ Multiples ☐ Swing ☐ Other:	

FASHION STYLE	
Personal Preference: ☐Professional ☐Business Casual ☐ Casual ☐ Athletic Wear ☐ Glam ☐ Minimalist ☐ Edgy	
Fit: ☐ Tailored ☐ Figure-Hugging ☐ Skin Tight ☐ Loose ☐ Baggy ☐ Skimpy	

RELATIONSHIPS	
Family Structure:	☐ Close Knit ☐ Estranged ☐ Absent ☐ Unknown
Favorite Relative:	
Closest Friend:	
Relationship History:	
As a Neighbor:	☐ Reclusive ☐ Friendly (knows their names) ☐ Knows by Sight Only ☐ No neighbors
NOTES:	

Support Character # 6

First Name:		Last Name:	
Birth Month:		Age:	

Relationship to Protagonist: ☐ Sibling ☐ Friend ☐ Love Interest
☐ Spouse ☐ Ex-lover ☐ Child ☐ Parent ☐ Relative
☐ Coworker. ☐ Boss/Supervisor ☐ Teacher/Mentor ☐ Employee
☐ Neighbor ☐ Leader ☐ Other:

Sexual Identity: ☐ Male ☐ Female ☐ Transgender ☐ Nonbinary

Race: ☐ White ☐ Black ☐ Native American ☐ Asian
☐ Pacific Islander ☐ Mixed Race ☐ Hispanic:

Ethnicity/ Ancestry:		Religion:	

Species: ☐ Human ☐ Vampire ☐ Shifter ☐ Fae ☐ Ghost
☐ Mythological god ☐ Witch/Mage ☐ Demon ☐ Angels ☐ Alien
☐ Mermaid ☐ Djinn ☐ Gargoyles ☐ Cyborg ☐ Monster
☐ AI (Artificial Intelligence)

Education: ☐ PhD ☐ Masters ☐ 4-year ☐ 2-year ☐ Tech Program
☐ High School Graduate ☐ GED ☐ Drop Out

Languages Spoken: ☐ English ☐ Mandarin ☐ Hindi ☐ Spanish
☐ French ☐ Arabic ☐ Russian ☐ ASL

Dialect/Accent:

Marital Status: ☐ Single ☐ Married ☐ Widowed
☐ Divorced ☐ Separated ☐ Polygamist

Occupation:		Employer:	
Skills/Hobbies:		Pets:	

Military: ☐ Never Served ☐ Active Duty ☐ Retired
☐ Honorable Discharge ☐ Dishonorable Discharge

Branch Served:		Rank/ Title:	

Socioeconomic Status: ☐ Top 2% ☐ High Class ☐ Upper Middle Class
☐ Lower Middle Class ☐ Lower Class ☐ Poor/Destitute

Criminal Record: ☐ None ☐ Misdemeanor ☐ Felony

Notes, Research, Links

DESCRIPTION			
Height:		**Weight:**	
Eye Color:		**Hair Color:**	
Complexion / Skin Tone:			
Hair Texture:		**Hair Length:**	

Shape of Face: ☐ Square ☐ Oval ☐ Rectangle/Oblong ☐ Round
☐ Diamond ☐ Triangle

Distinguishing Marks:		**Tattoos:**	

Vision: ☐ 20/20 ☐ Glasses ☐ Contacts ☐ Blind
☐ Astigmatism ☐ Nearsighted ☐ Farsighted ☐ Cataracts

Physical Limitations:		**Mental Limitations:**	
Medical Conditions:		**Allergies:**	

Body Type: ☐ Ectomorph ☐ Mesomorph ☐ Endomorph

Body Shape (female): ☐ Rectangle/Straight ☐ Apple ☐ Pear/Triangle ☐ Hourglass

Bust Size: ☐ AA ☐ A ☐ B ☐ C ☐ D ☐ DD ☐ E ☐ F ☐ G ☐ Larger

BACKGROUND			
Native Country:		**Native Language:**	
State/ Provence:		**City / Town:**	

Childhood Home: ☐ Single Family ☐ Townhome ☐ Apartment/Condo
☐ Mobile Home ☐ Farm ☐ Ranch
☐ Multiple Residences/Homes ☐ Homeless

Raised by: ☐ Both Parents ☐ Single Parent ☐ Relative
☐ Foster Care ☐ Orphan ☐ Adopted ☐ Non-Relative

Birth Order: ☐ Oldest ☐ Middle ☐ Youngest ☐ Twin

Parent Name:		**Parent Name:**	
Parent Occupation:		**Parent Occupation:**	
Number of Siblings:			
Sibling Names:			

Notes, Research, Links

PERSONALITY

Personality Type: ☐ Introvert ☐ Extrovert

Demeanor/Temperament:

☐ Friendly	☐ Cheerful	☐ Arrogant/Haughty	☐ Reserved
☐ Down to Earth	☐ Stoic	☐ Self-Absorbed	☐ Brooding
☐ Laidback	☐ Uptight	☐ Excitable	☐ Surly

Character Trait: ☐ Hero ☐ Antihero ☐ Villain ☐ Martyr ☐ Victim

Communication Style: ☐ Nonverbal ☐ Monosyllabic ☐ Articulate
☐ Speaks only when spoken to ☐ Gregarious ☐ Sign Language

Phobias:

Quirks:

Unhealthy Habits: ☐ Tobacco ☐ Alcohol ☐ Drugs ☐ Sex

Strengths/Weaknesses:

Closely Held Secret:

SEXUALITY

Sexual Partner Preference: ☐ Heterosexual ☐ Homosexual
☐ Bisexual ☐ Asexual ☐ Other:

Sexual Experience: ☐ Virgin ☐ Novice ☐ Experienced

Type of Sex Preferred: ☐ Vanilla/Traditional ☐ BDSM ☐ Kink ☐ Multiples
☐ Swing ☐ Other:

FASHION STYLE

Personal Preference: ☐ Professional ☐ Business Casual ☐ Casual
☐ Athletic Wear ☐ Glam ☐ Minimalist ☐ Edgy

Fit: ☐ Tailored ☐ Figure-Hugging ☐ Skin Tight
☐ Loose ☐ Baggy ☐ Skimpy

RELATIONSHIPS

Family Structure: ☐ Close Knit ☐ Estranged ☐ Absent ☐ Unknown

Favorite Relative:

Closest Friend:

Relationship History:

As a Neighbor: ☐ Reclusive ☐ Friendly (knows their names)
☐ Knows by Sight Only ☐ No neighbors

NOTES:

Support Character # 7

First Name:		Last Name:	

Birth Month:		Age:	

Relationship to Protagonist: ☐ Sibling ☐ Friend ☐ Love Interest
☐ Spouse ☐ Ex-lover ☐ Child ☐ Parent ☐ Relative
☐ Coworker. ☐ Boss/Supervisor ☐ Teacher/Mentor ☐ Employee
☐ Neighbor ☐ Leader ☐ Other:

Sexual Identity: ☐ Male ☐ Female ☐ Transgender ☐ Nonbinary

Race: ☐ White ☐ Black ☐ Native American ☐ Asian
☐ Pacific Islander ☐ Mixed Race ☐ Hispanic:

Ethnicity/ Ancestry:		Religion:	

Species: ☐ Human ☐ Vampire ☐ Shifter ☐ Fae ☐ Ghost
☐ Mythological god ☐ Witch/Mage ☐ Demon ☐ Angels ☐ Alien
☐ Mermaid ☐ Djinn ☐ Gargoyles ☐ Cyborg ☐ Monster
☐ AI (Artificial Intelligence)

Education: ☐ PhD ☐ Masters ☐ 4-year ☐ 2-year ☐ Tech Program
☐ High School Graduate ☐ GED ☐ Drop Out

Languages Spoken: ☐ English ☐ Mandarin ☐ Hindi ☐ Spanish
☐ French ☐ Arabic ☐ Russian ☐ ASL

Dialect/Accent:

Marital Status: ☐ Single ☐ Married ☐ Widowed
☐ Divorced ☐ Separated ☐ Polygamist

Occupation:		Employer:	

Skills/Hobbies:		Pets:	

Military: ☐ Never Served ☐ Active Duty ☐ Retired
☐ Honorable Discharge ☐ Dishonorable Discharge

Branch Served:		Rank/ Title:	

Socioeconomic Status: ☐ Top 2% ☐ High Class ☐ Upper Middle Class
☐ Lower Middle Class ☐ Lower Class ☐ Poor/Destitute

Criminal Record: ☐ None ☐ Misdemeanor ☐ Felony

Notes, Research, Links

DESCRIPTION			
Height:		**Weight:**	
Eye Color:		**Hair Color:**	
Complexion / Skin Tone:			
Hair Texture:		**Hair Length:**	

Shape of Face: ☐ Square ☐ Oval ☐ Rectangle/Oblong ☐ Round ☐ Diamond ☐ Triangle

Distinguishing Marks:		**Tattoos:**	

Vision: ☐ 20/20 ☐ Glasses ☐ Contacts ☐ Blind ☐ Astigmatism ☐ Nearsighted ☐ Farsighted ☐ Cataracts

Physical Limitations:		**Mental Limitations:**	
Medical Conditions:		**Allergies:**	

Body Type: ☐ Ectomorph ☐ Mesomorph ☐ Endomorph

Body Shape (female): ☐ Rectangle/Straight ☐ Apple ☐ Pear/Triangle ☐ Hourglass

Bust Size: ☐ AA ☐ A ☐ B ☐ C ☐ D ☐ DD ☐ E ☐ F ☐ G ☐ Larger

BACKGROUND			
Native Country:		**Native Language:**	
State/ Provence:		**City / Town:**	

Childhood Home: ☐ Single Family ☐ Townhome ☐ Apartment/Condo ☐ Mobile Home ☐ Farm ☐ Ranch ☐ Multiple Residences/Homes ☐ Homeless

Raised by: ☐ Both Parents ☐ Single Parent ☐ Relative ☐ Foster Care ☐ Orphan ☐ Adopted ☐ Non-Relative

Birth Order: ☐ Oldest ☐ Middle ☐ Youngest ☐ Twin

Parent Name:		**Parent Name:**	
Parent Occupation:		**Parent Occupation:**	

Number of Siblings:

Sibling Names:

Notes, Research, Links

PERSONALITY		
Personality Type:	☐ Introvert	☐ Extrovert

Demeanor/Temperament:			
☐ Friendly	☐ Cheerful	☐ Arrogant/Haughty	☐ Reserved
☐ Down to Earth	☐ Stoic	☐ Self-Absorbed	☐ Brooding
☐ Laidback	☐ Uptight	☐ Excitable	☐ Surly

Character Trait:	☐ Hero	☐ Antihero	☐ Villain	☐ Martyr	☐ Victim

Communication Style: ☐ Nonverbal ☐ Monosyllabic ☐ Articulate
☐ Speaks only when spoken to ☐ Gregarious ☐ Sign Language

Phobias:

Quirks:

Unhealthy Habits: ☐ Tobacco ☐ Alcohol ☐ Drugs ☐ Sex

Strengths/Weaknesses:	
Closely Held Secret:	

SEXUALITY	

Sexual Partner Preference: ☐ Heterosexual ☐ Homosexual
☐ Bisexual ☐ Asexual ☐ Other:

Sexual Experience: ☐ Virgin ☐ Novice ☐ Experienced

Type of Sex Preferred: ☐ Vanilla/Traditional ☐ BDSM ☐ Kink ☐ Multiples
☐ Swing ☐ Other:

FASHION STYLE	

Personal Preference: ☐Professional ☐Business Casual ☐ Casual
☐ Athletic Wear ☐ Glam ☐ Minimalist ☐ Edgy

Fit: ☐ Tailored ☐ Figure-Hugging ☐ Skin Tight
☐ Loose ☐ Baggy ☐ Skimpy

RELATIONSHIPS	

Family Structure:	☐ Close Knit ☐ Estranged ☐ Absent ☐ Unknown
Favorite Relative:	
Closest Friend:	
Relationship History:	
As a Neighbor:	☐ Reclusive ☐ Friendly (knows their names) ☐ Knows by Sight Only ☐ No neighbors
NOTES:	

Support Character # 8

First Name:		Last Name:	
Birth Month:		Age:	

Relationship to Protagonist: ☐ Sibling ☐ Friend ☐ Love Interest
☐ Spouse ☐ Ex-lover ☐ Child ☐ Parent ☐ Relative
☐ Coworker. ☐ Boss/Supervisor ☐ Teacher/Mentor ☐ Employee
☐ Neighbor ☐ Leader ☐ Other:

Sexual Identity: ☐ Male ☐ Female ☐ Transgender ☐ Nonbinary

Race: ☐ White ☐ Black ☐ Native American ☐ Asian
☐ Pacific Islander ☐ Mixed Race ☐ Hispanic:

Ethnicity/ Ancestry:		Religion:	

Species: ☐ Human ☐ Vampire ☐ Shifter ☐ Fae ☐ Ghost
☐ Mythological god ☐ Witch/Mage ☐ Demon ☐ Angels ☐ Alien
☐ Mermaid ☐ Djinn ☐ Gargoyles ☐ Cyborg ☐ Monster
☐ AI (Artificial Intelligence)

Education: ☐ PhD ☐ Masters ☐ 4-year ☐ 2-year ☐ Tech Program
☐ High School Graduate ☐ GED ☐ Drop Out

Languages Spoken: ☐ English ☐ Mandarin ☐ Hindi ☐ Spanish
☐ French ☐ Arabic ☐ Russian ☐ ASL

Dialect/Accent:

Marital Status: ☐ Single ☐ Married ☐ Widowed
☐ Divorced ☐ Separated ☐ Polygamist

Occupation:		Employer:	
Skills/Hobbies:		Pets:	

Military: ☐ Never Served ☐ Active Duty ☐ Retired
☐ Honorable Discharge ☐ Dishonorable Discharge

Branch Served:		Rank/ Title:	

Socioeconomic Status: ☐ Top 2% ☐ High Class ☐ Upper Middle Class
☐ Lower Middle Class ☐ Lower Class ☐ Poor/Destitute

Criminal Record: ☐ None ☐ Misdemeanor ☐ Felony

Notes, Research, Links

DESCRIPTION			
Height:		**Weight:**	
Eye Color:		**Hair Color:**	
Complexion / Skin Tone:			
Hair Texture:		**Hair Length:**	

Shape of Face: ☐ Square ☐ Oval ☐ Rectangle/Oblong ☐ Round
☐ Diamond ☐ Triangle

Distinguishing Marks:		**Tattoos:**	

Vision: ☐ 20/20 ☐ Glasses ☐ Contacts ☐ Blind
☐ Astigmatism ☐ Nearsighted ☐ Farsighted ☐ Cataracts

Physical Limitations:		**Mental Limitations:**	
Medical Conditions:		**Allergies:**	

Body Type: ☐ Ectomorph ☐ Mesomorph ☐ Endomorph

Body Shape (female): ☐ Rectangle/Straight ☐ Apple ☐ Pear/Triangle ☐ Hourglass

Bust Size: ☐ AA ☐ A ☐ B ☐ C ☐ D ☐ DD ☐ E ☐ F ☐ G ☐ Larger

BACKGROUND			
Native Country:		**Native Language:**	
State/ Provence:		**City / Town:**	

Childhood Home: ☐ Single Family ☐ Townhome ☐ Apartment/Condo
☐ Mobile Home ☐ Farm ☐ Ranch
☐ Multiple Residences/Homes ☐ Homeless

Raised by: ☐ Both Parents ☐ Single Parent ☐ Relative
☐ Foster Care ☐ Orphan ☐ Adopted ☐ Non-Relative

Birth Order: ☐ Oldest ☐ Middle ☐ Youngest ☐ Twin

Parent Name:		**Parent Name:**	
Parent Occupation:		**Parent Occupation:**	

Number of Siblings:

Sibling Names:

Notes, Research, Links

PERSONALITY

Personality Type: ☐ Introvert   ☐ Extrovert

Demeanor/Temperament:

☐ Friendly	☐ Cheerful	☐ Arrogant/Haughty	☐ Reserved
☐ Down to Earth	☐ Stoic	☐ Self-Absorbed	☐ Brooding
☐ Laidback	☐ Uptight	☐ Excitable	☐ Surly

Character Trait: ☐ Hero   ☐ Antihero   ☐ Villain   ☐ Martyr   ☐ Victim

Communication Style: ☐ Nonverbal   ☐ Monosyllabic   ☐ Articulate
☐ Speaks only when spoken to   ☐ Gregarious   ☐ Sign Language

Phobias:

Quirks:

Unhealthy Habits: ☐ Tobacco   ☐ Alcohol   ☐ Drugs   ☐ Sex

Strengths/Weaknesses:

Closely Held Secret:

SEXUALITY

Sexual Partner Preference: ☐ Heterosexual   ☐ Homosexual
☐ Bisexual   ☐ Asexual   ☐ Other:

Sexual Experience: ☐ Virgin   ☐ Novice   ☐ Experienced

Type of Sex Preferred: ☐ Vanilla/Traditional   ☐ BDSM   ☐ Kink   ☐ Multiples
☐ Swing   ☐ Other:

FASHION STYLE

Personal Preference: ☐ Professional   ☐ Business Casual   ☐ Casual
☐ Athletic Wear   ☐ Glam   ☐ Minimalist   ☐ Edgy

Fit: ☐ Tailored   ☐ Figure-Hugging   ☐ Skin Tight
     ☐ Loose   ☐ Baggy   ☐ Skimpy

RELATIONSHIPS

Family Structure: ☐ Close Knit   ☐ Estranged   ☐ Absent   ☐ Unknown

Favorite Relative:

Closest Friend:

Relationship History:

As a Neighbor: ☐ Reclusive   ☐ Friendly (knows their names)
☐ Knows by Sight Only   ☐ No neighbors

NOTES:

Support Character # 9

First Name:		Last Name:	
Birth Month:		Age:	

Relationship to Protagonist: ☐ Sibling ☐ Friend ☐ Love Interest
☐ Spouse ☐ Ex-lover ☐ Child ☐ Parent ☐ Relative
☐ Coworker. ☐ Boss/Supervisor ☐ Teacher/Mentor ☐ Employee
☐ Neighbor ☐ Leader ☐ Other:

Sexual Identity: ☐ Male ☐ Female ☐ Transgender ☐ Nonbinary

Race: ☐ White ☐ Black ☐ Native American ☐ Asian
☐ Pacific Islander ☐ Mixed Race ☐ Hispanic:

Ethnicity/ Ancestry:		Religion:	

Species: ☐ Human ☐ Vampire ☐ Shifter ☐ Fae ☐ Ghost
☐ Mythological god ☐ Witch/Mage ☐ Demon ☐ Angels ☐ Alien
☐ Mermaid ☐ Djinn ☐ Gargoyles ☐ Cyborg ☐ Monster
☐ AI (Artificial Intelligence)

Education: ☐ PhD ☐ Masters ☐ 4-year ☐ 2-year ☐ Tech Program
☐ High School Graduate ☐ GED ☐ Drop Out

Languages Spoken: ☐ English ☐ Mandarin ☐ Hindi ☐ Spanish
☐ French ☐ Arabic ☐ Russian ☐ ASL

Dialect/Accent:

Marital Status: ☐ Single ☐ Married ☐ Widowed
☐ Divorced ☐ Separated ☐ Polygamist

Occupation:		Employer:	
Skills/Hobbies:		Pets:	

Military: ☐ Never Served ☐ Active Duty ☐ Retired
☐ Honorable Discharge ☐ Dishonorable Discharge

Branch Served:		Rank/ Title:	

Socioeconomic Status: ☐ Top 2% ☐ High Class ☐ Upper Middle Class
☐ Lower Middle Class ☐ Lower Class ☐ Poor/Destitute

Criminal Record: ☐ None ☐ Misdemeanor ☐ Felony

Notes, Research, Links

DESCRIPTION			
Height:		**Weight:**	
Eye Color:		**Hair Color:**	
Complexion / Skin Tone:			
Hair Texture:		**Hair Length:**	

Shape of Face: ☐ Square ☐ Oval ☐ Rectangle/Oblong ☐ Round
☐ Diamond ☐ Triangle

Distinguishing Marks:		**Tattoos:**	

Vision: ☐ 20/20 ☐ Glasses ☐ Contacts ☐ Blind
☐ Astigmatism ☐ Nearsighted ☐ Farsighted ☐ Cataracts

Physical Limitations:		**Mental Limitations:**	
Medical Conditions:		**Allergies:**	

Body Type: ☐ Ectomorph ☐ Mesomorph ☐ Endomorph

Body Shape (female): ☐ Rectangle/Straight ☐ Apple ☐ Pear/Triangle ☐ Hourglass

Bust Size: ☐ AA ☐ A ☐ B ☐ C ☐ D ☐ DD ☐ E ☐ F ☐ G ☐ Larger

BACKGROUND			
Native Country:		**Native Language:**	
State/ Provence:		**City / Town:**	

Childhood Home: ☐ Single Family ☐ Townhome ☐ Apartment/Condo
☐ Mobile Home ☐ Farm ☐ Ranch
☐ Multiple Residences/Homes ☐ Homeless

Raised by: ☐ Both Parents ☐ Single Parent ☐ Relative
☐ Foster Care ☐ Orphan ☐ Adopted ☐ Non-Relative

Birth Order: ☐ Oldest ☐ Middle ☐ Youngest ☐ Twin

Parent Name:		**Parent Name:**	
Parent Occupation:		**Parent Occupation:**	

Number of Siblings:

Sibling Names:

Notes, Research, Links

PERSONALITY

Personality Type: ☐ Introvert   ☐ Extrovert

Demeanor/Temperament:

☐ Friendly	☐ Cheerful	☐ Arrogant/Haughty	☐ Reserved
☐ Down to Earth	☐ Stoic	☐ Self-Absorbed	☐ Brooding
☐ Laidback	☐ Uptight	☐ Excitable	☐ Surly

Character Trait: ☐ Hero   ☐ Antihero   ☐ Villain   ☐ Martyr   ☐ Victim

Communication Style: ☐ Nonverbal   ☐ Monosyllabic   ☐ Articulate
☐ Speaks only when spoken to   ☐ Gregarious   ☐ Sign Language

Phobias:

Quirks:

Unhealthy Habits: ☐ Tobacco   ☐ Alcohol   ☐ Drugs   ☐ Sex

Strengths/Weaknesses:	
Closely Held Secret:	

SEXUALITY

Sexual Partner Preference: ☐ Heterosexual   ☐ Homosexual
☐ Bisexual   ☐ Asexual   ☐ Other:

Sexual Experience: ☐ Virgin   ☐ Novice   ☐ Experienced

Type of Sex Preferred: ☐ Vanilla/Traditional   ☐ BDSM   ☐ Kink   ☐ Multiples
☐ Swing   ☐ Other:

FASHION STYLE

Personal Preference: ☐ Professional   ☐ Business Casual   ☐ Casual
☐ Athletic Wear   ☐ Glam   ☐ Minimalist   ☐ Edgy

Fit: ☐ Tailored   ☐ Figure-Hugging   ☐ Skin Tight
☐ Loose   ☐ Baggy   ☐ Skimpy

RELATIONSHIPS

Family Structure:	☐ Close Knit ☐ Estranged ☐ Absent ☐ Unknown
Favorite Relative:	
Closest Friend:	
Relationship History:	
As a Neighbor:	☐ Reclusive ☐ Friendly (knows their names) ☐ Knows by Sight Only ☐ No neighbors
NOTES:	

Support Character # 10

First Name:		Last Name:	
Birth Month:		**Age:**	

Relationship to Protagonist: ☐ Sibling ☐ Friend ☐ Love Interest
☐ Spouse ☐ Ex-lover ☐ Child ☐ Parent ☐ Relative
☐ Coworker. ☐ Boss/Supervisor ☐ Teacher/Mentor ☐ Employee
☐ Neighbor ☐ Leader ☐ Other:

Sexual Identity: ☐ Male ☐ Female ☐ Transgender ☐ Nonbinary

Race: ☐ White ☐ Black ☐ Native American ☐ Asian
☐ Pacific Islander ☐ Mixed Race ☐ Hispanic:

Ethnicity/ Ancestry:		Religion:	

Species: ☐ Human ☐ Vampire ☐ Shifter ☐ Fae ☐ Ghost
☐ Mythological god ☐ Witch/Mage ☐ Demon ☐ Angels ☐ Alien
☐ Mermaid ☐ Djinn ☐ Gargoyles ☐ Cyborg ☐ Monster
☐ AI (Artificial Intelligence)

Education: ☐ PhD ☐ Masters ☐ 4-year ☐ 2-year ☐ Tech Program
☐ High School Graduate ☐ GED ☐ Drop Out

Languages Spoken: ☐ English ☐ Mandarin ☐ Hindi ☐ Spanish
☐ French ☐ Arabic ☐ Russian ☐ ASL

Dialect/Accent:

Marital Status: ☐ Single ☐ Married ☐ Widowed
☐ Divorced ☐ Separated ☐ Polygamist

Occupation:		Employer:	
Skills/Hobbies:		**Pets:**	

Military: ☐ Never Served ☐ Active Duty ☐ Retired
☐ Honorable Discharge ☐ Dishonorable Discharge

Branch Served:		Rank/ Title:	

Socioeconomic Status: ☐ Top 2% ☐ High Class ☐ Upper Middle Class
☐ Lower Middle Class ☐ Lower Class ☐ Poor/Destitute

Criminal Record: ☐ None ☐ Misdemeanor ☐ Felony

Notes, Research, Links

DESCRIPTION			
Height:		**Weight:**	
Eye Color:		**Hair Color:**	
Complexion / Skin Tone:			
Hair Texture:		**Hair Length:**	

Shape of Face: ☐ Square ☐ Oval ☐ Rectangle/Oblong ☐ Round ☐ Diamond ☐ Triangle

Distinguishing Marks:		**Tattoos:**	

Vision: ☐ 20/20 ☐ Glasses ☐ Contacts ☐ Blind
☐ Astigmatism ☐ Nearsighted ☐ Farsighted ☐ Cataracts

Physical Limitations:		**Mental Limitations:**	
Medical Conditions:		**Allergies:**	

Body Type: ☐ Ectomorph ☐ Mesomorph ☐ Endomorph

Body Shape (female): ☐ Rectangle/Straight ☐ Apple ☐ Pear/Triangle ☐ Hourglass

Bust Size: ☐ AA ☐ A ☐ B ☐ C ☐ D ☐ DD ☐ E ☐ F ☐ G ☐ Larger

BACKGROUND			
Native Country:		**Native Language:**	
State/ Provence:		**City / Town:**	

Childhood Home: ☐ Single Family ☐ Townhome ☐ Apartment/Condo
☐ Mobile Home ☐ Farm ☐ Ranch
☐ Multiple Residences/Homes ☐ Homeless

Raised by: ☐ Both Parents ☐ Single Parent ☐ Relative
☐ Foster Care ☐ Orphan ☐ Adopted ☐ Non-Relative

Birth Order: ☐ Oldest ☐ Middle ☐ Youngest ☐ Twin

Parent Name:		**Parent Name:**	
Parent Occupation:		**Parent Occupation:**	

Number of Siblings:

Sibling Names:

Notes, Research, Links

PERSONALITY

Personality Type: ☐ Introvert ☐ Extrovert

Demeanor/Temperament:

☐ Friendly ☐ Cheerful ☐ Arrogant/Haughty ☐ Reserved

☐ Down to Earth ☐ Stoic ☐ Self-Absorbed ☐ Brooding

☐ Laidback ☐ Uptight ☐ Excitable ☐ Surly

Character Trait: ☐ Hero ☐ Antihero ☐ Villain ☐ Martyr ☐ Victim

Communication Style: ☐ Nonverbal ☐ Monosyllabic ☐ Articulate

☐ Speaks only when spoken to ☐ Gregarious ☐ Sign Language

Phobias:

Quirks:

Unhealthy Habits: ☐ Tobacco ☐ Alcohol ☐ Drugs ☐ Sex

Strengths/Weaknesses:

Closely Held Secret:

SEXUALITY

Sexual Partner Preference: ☐ Heterosexual ☐ Homosexual

☐ Bisexual ☐ Asexual ☐ Other:

Sexual Experience: ☐ Virgin ☐ Novice ☐ Experienced

Type of Sex Preferred: ☐ Vanilla/Traditional ☐ BDSM ☐ Kink ☐ Multiples

☐ Swing ☐ Other:

FASHION STYLE

Personal Preference: ☐ Professional ☐ Business Casual ☐ Casual

☐ Athletic Wear ☐ Glam ☐ Minimalist ☐ Edgy

Fit: ☐ Tailored ☐ Figure-Hugging ☐ Skin Tight

☐ Loose ☐ Baggy ☐ Skimpy

RELATIONSHIPS

Family Structure: ☐ Close Knit ☐ Estranged ☐ Absent ☐ Unknown

Favorite Relative:

Closest Friend:

Relationship History:

As a Neighbor: ☐ Reclusive ☐ Friendly (knows their names)

☐ Knows by Sight Only ☐ No neighbors

NOTES:

Section 4:
Minor
Characters

Don't rule out the importance of minor characters. No man is an island. Unless your protagonist is a hermit, they will cross paths daily with a myriad of people. In romances, minor characters are a good way to show continuity across an interconnected series with differing protagonist couples.

Minor Characters

Name: | **Occupation:**

Relationship to Protagonist: ☐ Sibling ☐ Friend. ☐ Love Interest
☐ Acquaintance ☐ Ex-lover ☐ Relative ☐ Coworker. ☐ Boss/Supervisor
☐ Teacher/Mentor ☐ Employee ☐ Neighbor ☐ Leader ☐ Stranger

Race: ☐ White ☐ Native American ☐ Asian ☐ Pacific Islander
☐ Mixed Race ☐ Hispanic: ☐ Black

Distinguishing Marks: | **Tattoos:**

Minor Description:

Notes:

Name: | **Occupation:**

Relationship to Protagonist: ☐ Sibling ☐ Friend. ☐ Love Interest
☐ Acquaintance ☐ Ex-lover ☐ Relative ☐ Coworker. ☐ Boss/Supervisor
☐ Teacher/Mentor ☐ Employee ☐ Neighbor ☐ Leader ☐ Stranger

Race: ☐ White ☐ Native American ☐ Asian ☐ Pacific Islander
☐ Mixed Race ☐ Hispanic: ☐ Black

Distinguishing Marks: | **Tattoos:**

Minor Description:

Notes:

Minor Characters

Name:		Occupation:	

Relationship to Protagonist: ☐ Sibling ☐ Friend. ☐ Love Interest
☐ Acquaintance ☐ Ex-lover ☐ Relative ☐ Coworker. ☐ Boss/Supervisor
☐ Teacher/Mentor ☐ Employee ☐ Neighbor ☐ Leader ☐ Stranger

Race: ☐ White ☐ Native American ☐ Asian ☐ Pacific Islander
☐ Mixed Race ☐ Hispanic: ☐ Black

Distinguishing Marks:		Tattoos:	

Minor Description:

Notes:

Name:		Occupation:	

Relationship to Protagonist: ☐ Sibling ☐ Friend. ☐ Love Interest
☐ Acquaintance ☐ Ex-lover ☐ Relative ☐ Coworker. ☐ Boss/Supervisor
☐ Teacher/Mentor ☐ Employee ☐ Neighbor ☐ Leader ☐ Stranger

Race: ☐ White ☐ Native American ☐ Asian ☐ Pacific Islander
☐ Mixed Race ☐ Hispanic: ☐ Black

Distinguishing Marks:		Tattoos:	

Minor Description:

Notes:

Minor Characters

Name:		Occupation:	

Relationship to Protagonist: ☐ Sibling   ☐ Friend.   ☐ Love Interest
☐ Acquaintance   ☐ Ex-lover   ☐ Relative   ☐ Coworker.   ☐ Boss/Supervisor
☐ Teacher/Mentor   ☐ Employee   ☐ Neighbor   ☐ Leader   ☐ Stranger

Race: ☐ White   ☐ Native American   ☐ Asian   ☐ Pacific Islander
☐ Mixed Race   ☐ Hispanic: ☐ Black

Distinguishing Marks:		**Tattoos:**	

Minor Description:

Notes:

Name:		Occupation:	

Relationship to Protagonist: ☐ Sibling   ☐ Friend.   ☐ Love Interest
☐ Acquaintance   ☐ Ex-lover   ☐ Relative   ☐ Coworker.   ☐ Boss/Supervisor
☐ Teacher/Mentor   ☐ Employee   ☐ Neighbor   ☐ Leader   ☐ Stranger

Race: ☐ White   ☐ Native American   ☐ Asian   ☐ Pacific Islander
☐ Mixed Race   ☐ Hispanic: ☐ Black

Distinguishing Marks:		**Tattoos:**	

Minor Description:

Notes:

Minor Characters

Name:		Occupation:	

Relationship to Protagonist: ☐ Sibling ☐ Friend. ☐ Love Interest
☐ Acquaintance ☐ Ex-lover ☐ Relative ☐ Coworker. ☐ Boss/Supervisor
☐ Teacher/Mentor ☐ Employee ☐ Neighbor ☐ Leader ☐ Stranger

Race: ☐ White ☐ Native American ☐ Asian ☐ Pacific Islander
☐ Mixed Race ☐ Hispanic: ☐ Black

Distinguishing Marks:		Tattoos:	

Minor Description:

Notes:

Name:		Occupation:	

Relationship to Protagonist: ☐ Sibling ☐ Friend. ☐ Love Interest
☐ Acquaintance ☐ Ex-lover ☐ Relative ☐ Coworker. ☐ Boss/Supervisor
☐ Teacher/Mentor ☐ Employee ☐ Neighbor ☐ Leader ☐ Stranger

Race: ☐ White ☐ Native American ☐ Asian ☐ Pacific Islander
☐ Mixed Race ☐ Hispanic: ☐ Black

Distinguishing Marks:		Tattoos:	

Minor Description:

Notes:

Minor Characters

Name:		Occupation:	

Relationship to Protagonist: ☐ Sibling   ☐ Friend.   ☐ Love Interest
☐ Acquaintance   ☐ Ex-lover   ☐ Relative   ☐ Coworker.   ☐ Boss/Supervisor   ☐
Teacher/Mentor   ☐ Employee   ☐ Neighbor   ☐ Leader   ☐ Stranger

Race: ☐ White   ☐ Native American   ☐ Asian   ☐ Pacific Islander
☐ Mixed Race   ☐ Hispanic: ☐ Black

Distinguishing Marks:		Tattoos:	

Minor Description:

Notes:

Name:		Occupation:	

Relationship to Protagonist: ☐ Sibling   ☐ Friend.   ☐ Love Interest
☐ Acquaintance   ☐ Ex-lover   ☐ Relative   ☐ Coworker.   ☐ Boss/Supervisor   ☐
Teacher/Mentor   ☐ Employee   ☐ Neighbor   ☐ Leader   ☐ Stranger

Race: ☐ White   ☐ Native American   ☐ Asian   ☐ Pacific Islander
☐ Mixed Race   ☐ Hispanic: ☐ Black

Distinguishing Marks:		Tattoos:	

Minor Description:

Notes:

Minor Characters

Name:		Occupation:	

Relationship to Protagonist: ☐ Sibling ☐ Friend. ☐ Love Interest
☐ Acquaintance ☐ Ex-lover ☐ Relative ☐ Coworker. ☐ Boss/Supervisor
☐ Teacher/Mentor ☐ Employee ☐ Neighbor ☐ Leader ☐ Stranger

Race: ☐ White ☐ Native American ☐ Asian ☐ Pacific Islander
☐ Mixed Race ☐ Hispanic: ☐ Black

Distinguishing Marks:		**Tattoos:**	

Minor Description:

Notes:

Name:		Occupation:	

Relationship to Protagonist: ☐ Sibling ☐ Friend. ☐ Love Interest
☐ Acquaintance ☐ Ex-lover ☐ Relative ☐ Coworker. ☐ Boss/Supervisor
☐ Teacher/Mentor ☐ Employee ☐ Neighbor ☐ Leader ☐ Stranger

Race: ☐ White ☐ Native American ☐ Asian ☐ Pacific Islander
☐ Mixed Race ☐ Hispanic: ☐ Black

Distinguishing Marks:		**Tattoos:**	

Minor Description:

Notes:

Minor Characters

Name:		Occupation:	

Relationship to Protagonist: ☐ Sibling ☐ Friend. ☐ Love Interest
☐ Acquaintance ☐ Ex-lover ☐ Relative ☐ Coworker. ☐ Boss/Supervisor
☐ Teacher/Mentor ☐ Employee ☐ Neighbor ☐ Leader ☐ Stranger

Race: ☐ White ☐ Native American ☐ Asian ☐ Pacific Islander
☐ Mixed Race ☐ Hispanic: ☐ Black

Distinguishing Marks:		**Tattoos:**	

Minor Description:

Notes:

Name:		Occupation:	

Relationship to Protagonist: ☐ Sibling ☐ Friend. ☐ Love Interest
☐ Acquaintance ☐ Ex-lover ☐ Relative ☐ Coworker. ☐ Boss/Supervisor
☐ Teacher/Mentor ☐ Employee ☐ Neighbor ☐ Leader ☐ Stranger

Race: ☐ White ☐ Native American ☐ Asian ☐ Pacific Islander
☐ Mixed Race ☐ Hispanic: ☐ Black

Distinguishing Marks:		**Tattoos:**	

Minor Description:

Notes:

Minor Characters

Name: | **Occupation:**

Relationship to Protagonist: ☐ Sibling ☐ Friend. ☐ Love Interest
☐ Acquaintance ☐ Ex-lover ☐ Relative ☐ Coworker. ☐ Boss/Supervisor
☐ Teacher/Mentor ☐ Employee ☐ Neighbor ☐ Leader ☐ Stranger

Race: ☐ White ☐ Native American ☐ Asian ☐ Pacific Islander
☐ Mixed Race ☐ Hispanic: ☐ Black

Distinguishing Marks: | **Tattoos:**

Minor Description:

Notes:

Name: | **Occupation:**

Relationship to Protagonist: ☐ Sibling ☐ Friend. ☐ Love Interest
☐ Acquaintance ☐ Ex-lover ☐ Relative ☐ Coworker. ☐ Boss/Supervisor
☐ Teacher/Mentor ☐ Employee ☐ Neighbor ☐ Leader ☐ Stranger

Race: ☐ White ☐ Native American ☐ Asian ☐ Pacific Islander
☐ Mixed Race ☐ Hispanic: ☐ Black

Distinguishing Marks: | **Tattoos:**

Minor Description:

Notes:

Minor Characters

Name: | **Occupation:**

Relationship to Protagonist: ☐ Sibling ☐ Friend. ☐ Love Interest
☐ Acquaintance ☐ Ex-lover ☐ Relative ☐ Coworker. ☐ Boss/Supervisor
☐ Teacher/Mentor ☐ Employee ☐ Neighbor ☐ Leader ☐ Stranger

Race: ☐ White ☐ Native American ☐ Asian ☐ Pacific Islander
☐ Mixed Race ☐ Hispanic: ☐ Black

Distinguishing Marks: | **Tattoos:**

Minor Description:

Notes:

Name: | **Occupation:**

Relationship to Protagonist: ☐ Sibling ☐ Friend. ☐ Love Interest
☐ Acquaintance ☐ Ex-lover ☐ Relative ☐ Coworker. ☐ Boss/Supervisor
☐ Teacher/Mentor ☐ Employee ☐ Neighbor ☐ Leader ☐ Stranger

Race: ☐ White ☐ Native American ☐ Asian ☐ Pacific Islander
☐ Mixed Race ☐ Hispanic: ☐ Black

Distinguishing Marks: | **Tattoos:**

Minor Description:

Notes:

Minor Characters

Name:		Occupation:	

Relationship to Protagonist: ☐ Sibling ☐ Friend. ☐ Love Interest
☐ Acquaintance ☐ Ex-lover ☐ Relative ☐ Coworker. ☐ Boss/Supervisor
☐ Teacher/Mentor ☐ Employee ☐ Neighbor ☐ Leader ☐ Stranger

Race: ☐ White ☐ Native American ☐ Asian ☐ Pacific Islander
☐ Mixed Race ☐ Hispanic: ☐ Black

Distinguishing Marks:		Tattoos:	

Minor Description:

Notes:

Name:		Occupation:	

Relationship to Protagonist: ☐ Sibling ☐ Friend. ☐ Love Interest
☐ Acquaintance ☐ Ex-lover ☐ Relative ☐ Coworker. ☐ Boss/Supervisor
☐ Teacher/Mentor ☐ Employee ☐ Neighbor ☐ Leader ☐ Stranger

Race: ☐ White ☐ Native American ☐ Asian ☐ Pacific Islander
☐ Mixed Race ☐ Hispanic: ☐ Black

Distinguishing Marks:		Tattoos:	

Minor Description:

Notes:

As long as you have ideas, you can keep going. That's why writing fiction is so much fun: because you're moving people about, and making settings for them to move in, so there's always something there to keep working on.

Guy Davenport

Bonus

Worksheets

Section 1:
Children

Who hasn't read a fiction story with kids in it? Whether it's the protagonist's offspring or a minor character limited to one scene, children can be a fun addition.

Minor Children

Child's Name:		Age:	
Parent Name		Parent Name:	

Birth Order: ☐ Oldest ☐ Middle ☐ Youngest ☐ Twin/Multiples

Number of Siblings:

Sibling Names:

Raised by: ☐ Both Parents ☐ Single Parent ☐ Relative ☐ Foster Care ☐ Orphan ☐ Adopted ☐ Non-Relative

Sexual Identity: ☐ Male ☐ Female ☐ Transgender ☐ Nonbinary

Race: ☐ White ☐ Black ☐ Native American ☐ Asian ☐ Pacific Islander ☐ Hispanic ☐ Mixed Race

Ethnicity/ Ancestry:		Religion:	
School:		Grade:	

DESCRIPTION

Height:		Weight:	
Eye Color:		Hair Color:	

Complexion / Skin Tone:

Hair Texture:		Hair Length:	
Birth Marks:		Tattoos:	

Shape of Face: ☐ Square ☐ Oval ☐ Rectangle/Oblong ☐ Round ☐ Diamond ☐ Triangle

Vision: ☐ 20/20 ☐ Glasses ☐ Contacts ☐ Blind ☐ Astigmatism ☐ Nearsighted ☐ Farsighted

Physical Limitations:		Mental Limitations:	
Medical Conditions:		Allergies:	

PERSONALITY / DEVELOPMENT

Speech:	☐ Nonverbal ☐ Monosyllabic ☐ Age Appropriate ☐ Speaks only when spoken to ☐ Gregarious
Mobility:	☐ Nonmobile ☐ Mobile ☐ Wheelchair

Notes, Research, Links

Demeanor / Temperament: ☐ Friendly ☐ Bubbly ☐ Shy ☐ Reserved
☐ Practical ☐ Stoic ☐ Self-Absorbed ☐ Brooding ☐ Laidback
☐ Uptight ☐ Excitable ☐ Surly ☐ Antisocial ☐ Easily Worried
☐ Helpful ☐ Generous ☐ Brainy ☐ Techy ☐ Nerd ☐ Jock

Favorite Relative:		**Closest Friend:**	
Phobias:		**Quirks:**	

Strengths/ Weaknesses:	
Sports/ Hobbies	

Unhealthy Habits: ☐ Tobacco ☐ Alcohol ☐ Drugs ☐ Sex ☐ Food

NOTES

Minor Children

Child's Name:		Age:	
Parent Name		Parent Name:	

Birth Order: ☐ Oldest ☐ Middle ☐ Youngest ☐ Twin/Multiples

Number of Siblings:

Sibling Names:

Raised by: ☐ Both Parents ☐ Single Parent ☐ Relative ☐ Foster Care ☐ Orphan ☐ Adopted ☐ Non-Relative

Sexual Identity: ☐ Male ☐ Female ☐ Transgender ☐ Nonbinary

Race: ☐ White ☐ Black ☐ Native American ☐ Asian ☐ Pacific Islander ☐ Hispanic ☐ Mixed Race

Ethnicity/ Ancestry:		Religion:	
School:		Grade:	

DESCRIPTION

Height:		Weight:	
Eye Color:		Hair Color:	

Complexion / Skin Tone:

Hair Texture:		Hair Length:	
Birth Marks:		Tattoos:	

Shape of Face: ☐ Square ☐ Oval ☐ Rectangle/Oblong ☐ Round ☐ Diamond ☐ Triangle

Vision: ☐ 20/20 ☐ Glasses ☐ Contacts ☐ Blind ☐ Astigmatism ☐ Nearsighted ☐ Farsighted

Physical Limitations:		Mental Limitations:	
Medical Conditions:		Allergies:	

PERSONALITY / DEVELOPMENT

Speech:	☐ Nonverbal ☐ Monosyllabic ☐ Age Appropriate ☐ Speaks only when spoken to ☐ Gregarious
Mobility:	☐ Nonmobile ☐ Mobile ☐ Wheelchair

Notes, Research, Links

Demeanor / Temperament:	☐ Friendly	☐ Bubbly	☐ Shy	☐ Reserved
☐ Practical ☐ Stoic ☐ Self-Absorbed		☐ Brooding	☐ Laidback	
☐ Uptight ☐ Excitable ☐ Surly		☐ Antisocial	☐ Easily Worried	
☐ Helpful ☐ Generous ☐ Brainy		☐ Techy	☐ Nerd ☐ Jock	

Favorite Relative:		Closest Friend:	
Phobias:		Quirks:	

Strengths/ Weaknesses:	
Sports/ Hobbies	

Unhealthy Habits: ☐ Tobacco ☐ Alcohol ☐ Drugs ☐ Sex ☐ Food

NOTES

Minor Children

Child's Name:		Age:	
Parent Name		Parent Name:	

Birth Order: ☐ Oldest ☐ Middle ☐ Youngest ☐ Twin/Multiples
Number of Siblings:
Sibling Names:
Raised by: ☐ Both Parents ☐ Single Parent ☐ Relative   ☐ Foster Care ☐ Orphan ☐ Adopted ☐ Non-Relative
Sexual Identity: ☐ Male ☐ Female ☐ Transgender ☐ Nonbinary
Race: ☐ White ☐ Black ☐ Native American ☐ Asian   ☐ Pacific Islander ☐ Hispanic ☐ Mixed Race

Ethnicity/ Ancestry:		Religion:	
School:		Grade:	

DESCRIPTION			
Height:		Weight:	
Eye Color:		Hair Color:	
Complexion / Skin Tone:			
Hair Texture:		Hair Length:	
Birth Marks:		Tattoos:	

Shape of Face: ☐ Square ☐ Oval ☐ Rectangle/Oblong ☐ Round   ☐ Diamond ☐ Triangle
Vision: ☐ 20/20 ☐ Glasses ☐ Contacts ☐ Blind   ☐ Astigmatism ☐ Nearsighted ☐ Farsighted

Physical Limitations:		Mental Limitations:	
Medical Conditions:		Allergies:	

PERSONALITY / DEVELOPMENT	
Speech:	☐ Nonverbal ☐ Monosyllabic ☐ Age Appropriate ☐ Speaks only when spoken to ☐ Gregarious
Mobility:	☐ Nonmobile ☐ Mobile ☐ Wheelchair

Notes, Research, Links

Demeanor / Temperament:	☐ Friendly	☐ Bubbly	☐ Shy	☐ Reserved
☐ Practical ☐ Stoic ☐ Self-Absorbed ☐ Brooding ☐ Laidback				
☐ Uptight ☐ Excitable ☐ Surly ☐ Antisocial ☐ Easily Worried				
☐ Helpful ☐ Generous ☐ Brainy ☐ Techy ☐ Nerd ☐ Jock				

Favorite Relative:		Closest Friend:	
Phobias:		Quirks:	

Strengths/ Weaknesses:	
Sports/ Hobbies	

Unhealthy Habits: ☐ Tobacco ☐ Alcohol ☐ Drugs ☐ Sex ☐ Food

NOTES

Minor Children

Child's Name:		Age:	
Parent Name		Parent Name:	

Birth Order: ☐ Oldest ☐ Middle ☐ Youngest ☐ Twin/Multiples
Number of Siblings:
Sibling Names:
Raised by: ☐ Both Parents ☐ Single Parent ☐ Relative ☐ Foster Care ☐ Orphan ☐ Adopted ☐ Non-Relative
Sexual Identity: ☐ Male ☐ Female ☐ Transgender ☐ Nonbinary
Race: ☐ White ☐ Black ☐ Native American ☐ Asian ☐ Pacific Islander ☐ Hispanic ☐ Mixed Race

Ethnicity/ Ancestry:		Religion:	
School:		Grade:	

DESCRIPTION			
Height:		Weight:	
Eye Color:		Hair Color:	

Complexion / Skin Tone:

Hair Texture:		Hair Length:	
Birth Marks:		Tattoos:	

Shape of Face: ☐ Square ☐ Oval ☐ Rectangle/Oblong ☐ Round ☐ Diamond ☐ Triangle
Vision: ☐ 20/20 ☐ Glasses ☐ Contacts ☐ Blind ☐ Astigmatism ☐ Nearsighted ☐ Farsighted

Physical Limitations:		Mental Limitations:	
Medical Conditions:		Allergies:	

PERSONALITY / DEVELOPMENT	
Speech:	☐ Nonverbal ☐ Monosyllabic ☐ Age Appropriate ☐ Speaks only when spoken to ☐ Gregarious
Mobility:	☐ Nonmobile ☐ Mobile ☐ Wheelchair

Notes, Research, Links

Demeanor / Temperament:	☐ Friendly	☐ Bubbly	☐ Shy	☐ Reserved
☐ Practical ☐ Stoic ☐ Self-Absorbed		☐ Brooding	☐ Laidback	
☐ Uptight ☐ Excitable ☐ Surly		☐ Antisocial	☐ Easily Worried	
☐ Helpful ☐ Generous ☐ Brainy		☐ Techy	☐ Nerd ☐ Jock	

Favorite Relative:		Closest Friend:	
Phobias:		Quirks:	

Strengths/ Weaknesses:	
Sports/ Hobbies	

Unhealthy Habits: ☐ Tobacco ☐ Alcohol ☐ Drugs ☐ Sex ☐ Food

NOTES

Minor Children

Child's Name:		Age:	
Parent Name		Parent Name:	

Birth Order: ☐ Oldest ☐ Middle ☐ Youngest ☐ Twin/Multiples

Number of Siblings:

Sibling Names:

Raised by: ☐ Both Parents ☐ Single Parent ☐ Relative
☐ Foster Care ☐ Orphan ☐ Adopted ☐ Non-Relative

Sexual Identity: ☐ Male ☐ Female ☐ Transgender ☐ Nonbinary

Race: ☐ White ☐ Black ☐ Native American ☐ Asian
☐ Pacific Islander ☐ Hispanic ☐ Mixed Race

Ethnicity/ Ancestry:		Religion:	
School:		Grade:	

DESCRIPTION

Height:		Weight:	
Eye Color:		Hair Color:	

Complexion / Skin Tone:

Hair Texture:		Hair Length:	
Birth Marks:		Tattoos:	

Shape of Face: ☐ Square ☐ Oval ☐ Rectangle/Oblong ☐ Round
☐ Diamond ☐ Triangle

Vision: ☐ 20/20 ☐ Glasses ☐ Contacts ☐ Blind
☐ Astigmatism ☐ Nearsighted ☐ Farsighted

Physical Limitations:		Mental Limitations:	
Medical Conditions:		Allergies:	

PERSONALITY / DEVELOPMENT

Speech:	☐ Nonverbal ☐ Monosyllabic ☐ Age Appropriate ☐ Speaks only when spoken to ☐ Gregarious
Mobility:	☐ Nonmobile ☐ Mobile ☐ Wheelchair

Notes, Research, Links

Demeanor / Temperament: ☐ Friendly ☐ Bubbly ☐ Shy ☐ Reserved
☐ Practical ☐ Stoic ☐ Self-Absorbed ☐ Brooding ☐ Laidback
☐ Uptight ☐ Excitable ☐ Surly ☐ Antisocial ☐ Easily Worried
☐ Helpful ☐ Generous ☐ Brainy ☐ Techy ☐ Nerd ☐ Jock

Favorite Relative:		**Closest Friend:**	
Phobias:		**Quirks:**	

Strengths/ Weaknesses:	
Sports/ Hobbies	

Unhealthy Habits: ☐ Tobacco ☐ Alcohol ☐ Drugs ☐ Sex ☐ Food

NOTES

Minor Children

Child's Name:		Age:	
Parent Name		Parent Name:	

Birth Order: ☐ Oldest ☐ Middle ☐ Youngest ☐ Twin/Multiples
Number of Siblings:
Sibling Names:
Raised by: ☐ Both Parents ☐ Single Parent ☐ Relative ☐ Foster Care ☐ Orphan ☐ Adopted ☐ Non-Relative
Sexual Identity: ☐ Male ☐ Female ☐ Transgender ☐ Nonbinary
Race: ☐ White ☐ Black ☐ Native American ☐ Asian ☐ Pacific Islander ☐ Hispanic ☐ Mixed Race

Ethnicity/ Ancestry:		Religion:	
School:		**Grade:**	

DESCRIPTION			
Height:		**Weight:**	
Eye Color:		**Hair Color:**	

Complexion / Skin Tone:

Hair Texture:		Hair Length:	
Birth Marks:		**Tattoos:**	

Shape of Face: ☐ Square ☐ Oval ☐ Rectangle/Oblong ☐ Round ☐ Diamond ☐ Triangle
Vision: ☐ 20/20 ☐ Glasses ☐ Contacts ☐ Blind ☐ Astigmatism ☐ Nearsighted ☐ Farsighted

Physical Limitations:		Mental Limitations:	
Medical Conditions:		**Allergies:**	

PERSONALITY / DEVELOPMENT	
Speech:	☐ Nonverbal ☐ Monosyllabic ☐ Age Appropriate ☐ Speaks only when spoken to ☐ Gregarious
Mobility:	☐ Nonmobile ☐ Mobile ☐ Wheelchair

Notes, Research, Links

Demeanor / Temperament: ☐ Friendly   ☐ Bubbly   ☐ Shy   ☐ Reserved
☐ Practical   ☐ Stoic   ☐ Self-Absorbed   ☐ Brooding   ☐ Laidback
☐ Uptight   ☐ Excitable   ☐ Surly   ☐ Antisocial   ☐ Easily Worried
☐ Helpful   ☐ Generous   ☐ Brainy   ☐ Techy   ☐ Nerd   ☐ Jock

Favorite Relative:		Closest Friend:	
Phobias:		Quirks:	

Strengths/ Weaknesses:	
Sports/ Hobbies	

Unhealthy Habits: ☐ Tobacco   ☐ Alcohol   ☐ Drugs   ☐ Sex   ☐ Food

NOTES

Section 2:
Animal Companions

It might seem strange to have a worksheets dedicated to pets, but if you're a pet owner, you know our furry friends have personalities of their own. Readers love reading about animals. They bring a little something extra to the plot.

Owner:

Pet Name:

Pet Type: ☐ Dog ☐ Cat ☐ Bird
☐ Pig ☐ Fish ☐ Hamster/Gerbil
☐ Snake ☐ Rabbit ☐ Horse
☐ Iguana ☐ Ferret ☐ Mice
☐ Turtle/Frog ☐ Dragon

Breed:

Description:

Temperament: ☐ Calm ☐ Lazy ☐ Hyper ☐ Scary ☐ Friendly ☐ Aggressive ☐ Antisocial

Notes:

Owner:

Pet Name:

Pet Type: ☐ Dog ☐ Cat ☐ Bird
☐ Pig ☐ Fish ☐ Hamster/Gerbil
☐ Snake ☐ Rabbit ☐ Horse
☐ Iguana ☐ Ferret ☐ Mice
☐ Turtle/Frog ☐ Dragon

Breed:

Description:

Temperament: ☐ Calm ☐ Lazy
☐ Hyper ☐ Scary ☐ Friendly
☐ Aggressive ☐ Antisocial

Notes:

Owner:

Pet Name:

Pet Type: ☐ Dog ☐ Cat ☐ Bird
☐ Pig ☐ Fish ☐ Hamster/Gerbil
☐ Snake ☐ Rabbit ☐ Horse
☐ Iguana ☐ Ferret ☐ Mice
☐ Turtle/Frog ☐ Dragon

Breed:

Description:

Temperament: ☐ Calm ☐ Lazy ☐ Hyper ☐ Scary ☐ Friendly ☐ Aggressive ☐ Antisocial

Notes:

Owner:

Pet Name:

Pet Type: ☐ Dog ☐ Cat ☐ Bird
☐ Pig ☐ Fish ☐ Hamster/Gerbil
☐ Snake ☐ Rabbit ☐ Horse
☐ Iguana ☐ Ferret ☐ Mice
☐ Turtle/Frog ☐ Dragon

Breed:

Description:

Temperament: ☐ Calm ☐ Lazy
☐ Hyper ☐ Scary ☐ Friendly
☐ Aggressive ☐ Antisocial

Notes:

Owner:

Pet Name:

Pet Type: ☐ Dog ☐ Cat ☐ Bird
☐ Pig ☐ Fish ☐ Hamster/Gerbil
☐ Snake ☐ Rabbit ☐ Horse
☐ Iguana ☐ Ferret ☐ Mice
☐ Turtle/Frog ☐ Dragon

Breed:

Description:

Temperament: ☐ Calm ☐ Lazy ☐ Hyper ☐ Scary ☐ Friendly ☐ Aggressive ☐ Antisocial

Notes:

Owner:

Pet Name:

Pet Type: ☐ Dog ☐ Cat ☐ Bird
☐ Pig ☐ Fish ☐ Hamster/Gerbil
☐ Snake ☐ Rabbit ☐ Horse
☐ Iguana ☐ Ferret ☐ Mice
☐ Turtle/Frog ☐ Dragon

Breed:

Description:

Temperament: ☐ Calm ☐ Lazy
☐ Hyper ☐ Scary ☐ Friendly
☐ Aggressive ☐ Antisocial

Notes:

Owner:

Pet Name:

Pet Type: ☐ Dog ☐ Cat ☐ Bird
☐ Pig ☐ Fish ☐ Hamster/Gerbil
☐ Snake ☐ Rabbit ☐ Horse
☐ Iguana ☐ Ferret ☐ Mice
☐ Turtle/Frog ☐ Dragon

Breed:

Description:

Temperament: ☐ Calm ☐ Lazy
☐ Hyper ☐ Scary ☐ Friendly
☐ Aggressive ☐ Antisocial

Notes:

Owner:

Pet Name:

Pet Type: ☐ Dog ☐ Cat ☐ Bird
☐ Pig ☐ Fish ☐ Hamster/Gerbil
☐ Snake ☐ Rabbit ☐ Horse
☐ Iguana ☐ Ferret ☐ Mice
☐ Turtle/Frog ☐ Dragon

Breed:

Description:

Temperament: ☐ Calm ☐ Lazy
☐ Hyper ☐ Scary ☐ Friendly
☐ Aggressive ☐ Antisocial

Notes:

Owner:	Owner:
Pet Name:	**Pet Name:**
Pet Type: ☐ Dog ☐ Cat ☐ Bird ☐ Pig ☐ Fish ☐ Hamster/Gerbil ☐ Snake ☐ Rabbit ☐ Horse ☐ Iguana ☐ Ferret ☐ Mice ☐ Turtle/Frog ☐ Dragon	**Pet Type:** ☐ Dog ☐ Cat ☐ Bird ☐ Pig ☐ Fish ☐ Hamster/Gerbil ☐ Snake ☐ Rabbit ☐ Horse ☐ Iguana ☐ Ferret ☐ Mice ☐ Turtle/Frog ☐ Dragon
Breed:	**Breed:**
Description:	**Description:**
Temperament: ☐ Calm ☐ Lazy ☐ Hyper ☐ Scary ☐ Friendly ☐ Aggressive ☐ Antisocial	**Temperament:** ☐ Calm ☐ Lazy ☐ Hyper ☐ Scary ☐ Friendly ☐ Aggressive ☐ Antisocial
Notes:	**Notes:**

Owner:	Owner:
Pet Name:	**Pet Name:**
Pet Type: ☐ Dog ☐ Cat ☐ Bird ☐ Pig ☐ Fish ☐ Hamster/Gerbil ☐ Snake ☐ Rabbit ☐ Horse ☐ Iguana ☐ Ferret ☐ Mice ☐ Turtle/Frog ☐ Dragon	**Pet Type:** ☐ Dog ☐ Cat ☐ Bird ☐ Pig ☐ Fish ☐ Hamster/Gerbil ☐ Snake ☐ Rabbit ☐ Horse ☐ Iguana ☐ Ferret ☐ Mice ☐ Turtle/Frog ☐ Dragon
Breed:	**Breed:**
Description:	**Description:**
Temperament: ☐ Calm ☐ Lazy ☐ Hyper ☐ Scary ☐ Friendly ☐ Aggressive ☐ Antisocial	**Temperament:** ☐ Calm ☐ Lazy ☐ Hyper ☐ Scary ☐ Friendly ☐ Aggressive ☐ Antisocial
Notes:	**Notes:**

Additional Protagonists

This section is for authors who write menages and reverse harems.

Protagonist # 7

First Name:		Last Name:	
Name Meaning:		Name Meaning:	
Birth Month:		Age:	

Sexual Identity: ☐ Male ☐ Female ☐ Transgender ☐ Nonbinary

Race: ☐ White ☐ Black ☐ Native American ☐ Asian
☐ Pacific Islander ☐ Hispanic ☐ Mixed Race

Ethnicity/ Ancestry:		Religion:	

Species: ☐ Human ☐ Alien ☐ Vampire ☐ Shifter ☐ Fae
☐ Ghost ☐ Mythological god ☐ Witch/Mage ☐ Demon
☐ Mermaid ☐ Djinn ☐ Angels ☐ Gargoyles ☐ Cyborg

Education: ☐ PhD ☐ Masters ☐ 4-year ☐ 2-year ☐ Technical School
☐ High School Graduate ☐ GED ☐ HS Drop Out

Languages: ☐ English ☐ Mandarin ☐ Hindi ☐ Spanish
☐ French ☐ Arabic ☐ Russian ☐ ASL

Dialect/Accent:

Marital Status: ☐ Single ☐ Married ☐ Widowed
☐ Divorced ☐ Separated ☐ Polygamist

Skills/ Hobbies:		Pets:	

Socioeconomic Status: ☐ Top 2% ☐ Wealthy ☐ Poor
☐ Upper Middle Class ☐ Middle Class ☐ Lower Class

Occupation		Employer	

Military: ☐ Never Served ☐ Active Duty ☐ Retired
☐ Honorable Discharge ☐ Dishonorable Discharge

Branch Served:		Years Served:	

Rank/Title:

Criminal Record: ☐ None ☐ Misdemeanor ☐ Felony

DESCRIPTION

Height:		**Weight:**	
Eye Color:		**Hair Color:**	

Complexion / Skin Tone:

Hair Texture:		**Hair Length:**	

Shape of Face: ☐ Square ☐ Oval ☐ Rectangle/Oblong ☐ Round
☐ Diamond ☐ Triangle

Distinguishing Marks:		**Tattoos:**	

Vision: ☐ 20/20 ☐ Glasses ☐ Contacts ☐ Blind
☐ Astigmatism ☐ Nearsighted ☐ Farsighted ☐ Cataracts

Physical Limitations:		**Mental Limitations:**	
Medical Conditions:		**Allergies:**	

Body Type: ☐ Ectomorph ☐ Mesomorph ☐ Endomorph

Body Shape (female): ☐ Rectangle/Straight ☐ Apple
☐ Pear/Triangle ☐ Hourglass

Bust Size: ☐ AA ☐ A ☐ B ☐ C ☐ D ☐ DD ☐ E ☐ F ☐ G ☐ Larger

BACKGROUND

Native Country:		**Native Language:**	
State/ Provence:		**City / Town:**	

Childhood Home: ☐ Single Family ☐ Townhome ☐ Apartment/Condo
☐ Mobile Home ☐ Farm ☐ Ranch
☐ Multiple Residences/Homes ☐ Homeless

Raised by: ☐ Both Parents ☐ Single Parent ☐ Relative
☐ Foster Care ☐ Orphan ☐ Adopted ☐ Non-Relative

Birth Order: ☐ Oldest ☐ Middle ☐ Youngest ☐ Twin

Parent Name:		**Parent Name:**	
Parent Occupation:		**Parent Occupation:**	

Number of Siblings:

Sibling Names:

PERSONALITY		
Personality Type:	☐ Introvert	☐ Extrovert

Demeanor/Temperament:			
☐ Friendly	☐ Cheerful	☐ Arrogant/Haughty	☐ Reserved
☐ Down to Earth	☐ Stoic	☐ Self-Absorbed	☐ Brooding
☐ Laidback	☐ Uptight	☐ Excitable	☐ Surly

Character Trait:	☐ Hero	☐ Antihero	☐ Villain
	☐ Martyr	☐ Victim	

Communication Style: ☐ Nonverbal ☐ Monosyllabic ☐ Normal
☐ Speaks only when spoken to ☐ Gregarious ☐ Sign Language

Phobias:

Quirks:

Unhealthy Habits: ☐ Tobacco ☐ Alcohol ☐ Drugs

Strengths/Weaknesses:

Closely Held Secret:

SEXUALITY

Sexual Partner Preference: ☐ Heterosexual ☐ Homosexual
☐ Bisexual ☐ Asexual ☐ Other:

Sexual Experience:
☐ Virgin ☐ Novice ☐ Experienced

Type of Sex Preferred:
☐ Vanilla/Traditional ☐ BDSM ☐ Kink ☐ Multiples ☐ Swing
☐ Other:

FASHION STYLE

Personal Preference: ☐Professional ☐Business Casual ☐ Casual
☐ Athletic Wear ☐ Glam ☐ Minimalist ☐ Edgy

Fit: ☐ Tailored ☐ Figure-Hugging ☐ Skin Tight
☐ Loose ☐ Baggy ☐ Skimpy

RELATIONSHIPS

Family Structure: ☐ Close Knit ☐ Estranged ☐ Absent ☐ Unknown

Favorite Relative:

Closest Friend:

Work Buddy/Spouse:

As a Neighbor: ☐ Reclusive ☐ Friendly (knows their names)
☐ Knows by Sight Only ☐ No neighbors

Protagonist # 8

First Name:		Last Name:	
Name Meaning:		Name Meaning:	
Birth Month:		Age:	

Sexual Identity: ☐ Male ☐ Female ☐ Transgender ☐ Nonbinary

Race: ☐ White ☐ Black ☐ Native American ☐ Asian
☐ Pacific Islander ☐ Hispanic ☐ Mixed Race

Ethnicity/ Ancestry:		Religion:	

Species: ☐ Human ☐ Alien ☐ Vampire ☐ Shifter ☐ Fae
☐ Ghost ☐ Mythological god ☐ Witch/Mage ☐ Demon
☐ Mermaid ☐ Djinn ☐ Angels ☐ Gargoyles ☐ Cyborg

Education: ☐ PhD ☐ Masters ☐ 4-year ☐ 2-year ☐ Technical School
☐ High School Graduate ☐ GED ☐ HS Drop Out

Languages: ☐ English ☐ Mandarin ☐ Hindi ☐ Spanish
☐ French ☐ Arabic ☐ Russian ☐ ASL

Dialect/Accent:

Marital Status: ☐ Single ☐ Married ☐ Widowed
☐ Divorced ☐ Separated ☐ Polygamist

Skills/ Hobbies:		Pets:	

Socioeconomic Status: ☐ Top 2% ☐ Wealthy ☐ Poor
☐ Upper Middle Class ☐ Middle Class ☐ Lower Class

Occupation		Employer	

Military: ☐ Never Served ☐ Active Duty ☐ Retired
☐ Honorable Discharge ☐ Dishonorable Discharge

Branch Served:		Years Served:	

Rank/Title:

Criminal Record: ☐ None ☐ Misdemeanor ☐ Felony

DESCRIPTION			
Height:		**Weight:**	
Eye Color:		**Hair Color:**	
Complexion / Skin Tone:			
Hair Texture:		**Hair Length:**	

Shape of Face: ☐ Square ☐ Oval ☐ Rectangle/Oblong ☐ Round
☐ Diamond ☐ Triangle

Distinguishing Marks:		**Tattoos:**	

Vision: ☐ 20/20 ☐ Glasses ☐ Contacts ☐ Blind
☐ Astigmatism ☐ Nearsighted ☐ Farsighted ☐ Cataracts

Physical Limitations:		**Mental Limitations:**	
Medical Conditions:		**Allergies:**	

Body Type: ☐ Ectomorph ☐ Mesomorph ☐ Endomorph

Body Shape (female): ☐ Rectangle/Straight ☐ Apple
☐ Pear/Triangle ☐ Hourglass

Bust Size: ☐ AA ☐ A ☐ B ☐ C ☐ D ☐ DD ☐ E ☐ F ☐ G ☐ Larger

BACKGROUND			
Native Country:		**Native Language:**	
State/ Provence:		**City / Town:**	

Childhood Home: ☐ Single Family ☐ Townhome ☐ Apartment/Condo
☐ Mobile Home ☐ Farm ☐ Ranch
☐ Multiple Residences/Homes ☐ Homeless

Raised by: ☐ Both Parents ☐ Single Parent ☐ Relative
☐ Foster Care ☐ Orphan ☐ Adopted ☐ Non-Relative

Birth Order: ☐ Oldest ☐ Middle ☐ Youngest ☐ Twin

Parent Name:		**Parent Name:**	
Parent Occupation:		**Parent Occupation:**	
Number of Siblings:			
Sibling Names:			

PERSONALITY

Personality Type: ☐ Introvert ☐ Extrovert

Demeanor/Temperament:
☐ Friendly ☐ Cheerful ☐ Arrogant/Haughty ☐ Reserved
☐ Down to Earth ☐ Stoic ☐ Self-Absorbed ☐ Brooding
☐ Laidback ☐ Uptight ☐ Excitable ☐ Surly

Character Trait: ☐ Hero ☐ Antihero ☐ Villain
☐ Martyr ☐ Victim

Communication Style: ☐ Nonverbal ☐ Monosyllabic ☐ Normal
☐ Speaks only when spoken to ☐ Gregarious ☐ Sign Language

Phobias:

Quirks:

Unhealthy Habits: ☐ Tobacco ☐ Alcohol ☐ Drugs

Strengths/Weaknesses:

Closely Held Secret:

SEXUALITY

Sexual Partner Preference: ☐ Heterosexual ☐ Homosexual
☐ Bisexual ☐ Asexual ☐ Other:

Sexual Experience:
☐ Virgin ☐ Novice ☐ Experienced

Type of Sex Preferred:
☐ Vanilla/Traditional ☐ BDSM ☐ Kink ☐ Multiples ☐ Swing
☐ Other:

FASHION STYLE

Personal Preference: ☐ Professional ☐ Business Casual ☐ Casual
☐ Athletic Wear ☐ Glam ☐ Minimalist ☐ Edgy

Fit: ☐ Tailored ☐ Figure-Hugging ☐ Skin Tight
☐ Loose ☐ Baggy ☐ Skimpy

RELATIONSHIPS

Family Structure: ☐ Close Knit ☐ Estranged ☐ Absent ☐ Unknown

Favorite Relative:

Closest Friend:

Work Buddy/Spouse:

As a Neighbor: ☐ Reclusive ☐ Friendly (knows their names)
☐ Knows by Sight Only ☐ No neighbors

Protagonist # 9

First Name:		Last Name:	
Name Meaning:		Name Meaning:	
Birth Month:		Age:	

Sexual Identity: ☐ Male ☐ Female ☐ Transgender ☐ Nonbinary

Race: ☐ White ☐ Black ☐ Native American ☐ Asian
☐ Pacific Islander ☐ Hispanic ☐ Mixed Race

Ethnicity/ Ancestry:		Religion:	

Species: ☐ Human ☐ Alien ☐ Vampire ☐ Shifter ☐ Fae
☐ Ghost ☐ Mythological god ☐ Witch/Mage ☐ Demon
☐ Mermaid ☐ Djinn ☐ Angels ☐ Gargoyles ☐ Cyborg

Education: ☐ PhD ☐ Masters ☐ 4-year ☐ 2-year ☐ Technical School
☐ High School Graduate ☐ GED ☐ HS Drop Out

Languages: ☐ English ☐ Mandarin ☐ Hindi ☐ Spanish
☐ French ☐ Arabic ☐ Russian ☐ ASL

Dialect/Accent:

Marital Status: ☐ Single ☐ Married ☐ Widowed
☐ Divorced ☐ Separated ☐ Polygamist

Skills/ Hobbies:		Pets:	

Socioeconomic Status: ☐ Top 2% ☐ Wealthy ☐ Poor
☐ Upper Middle Class ☐ Middle Class ☐ Lower Class

Occupation		Employer	

Military: ☐ Never Served ☐ Active Duty ☐ Retired
☐ Honorable Discharge ☐ Dishonorable Discharge

Branch Served:		Years Served:	

Rank/Title:

Criminal Record: ☐ None ☐ Misdemeanor ☐ Felony

DESCRIPTION			
Height:		**Weight:**	
Eye Color:		**Hair Color:**	
Complexion / Skin Tone:			
Hair Texture:		**Hair Length:**	

Shape of Face: ☐ Square ☐ Oval ☐ Rectangle/Oblong ☐ Round
☐ Diamond ☐ Triangle

Distinguishing Marks:		**Tattoos:**	

Vision: ☐ 20/20 ☐ Glasses ☐ Contacts ☐ Blind
☐ Astigmatism ☐ Nearsighted ☐ Farsighted ☐ Cataracts

Physical Limitations:		**Mental Limitations:**	
Medical Conditions:		**Allergies:**	

Body Type: ☐ Ectomorph ☐ Mesomorph ☐ Endomorph

Body Shape (female): ☐ Rectangle/Straight ☐ Apple
☐ Pear/Triangle ☐ Hourglass

Bust Size: ☐ AA ☐ A ☐ B ☐ C ☐ D ☐ DD ☐ E ☐ F ☐ G ☐ Larger

BACKGROUND			
Native Country:		**Native Language:**	
State/ Provence:		**City / Town:**	

Childhood Home: ☐ Single Family ☐ Townhome ☐ Apartment/Condo
☐ Mobile Home ☐ Farm ☐ Ranch
☐ Multiple Residences/Homes ☐ Homeless

Raised by: ☐ Both Parents ☐ Single Parent ☐ Relative
☐ Foster Care ☐ Orphan ☐ Adopted ☐ Non-Relative

Birth Order: ☐ Oldest ☐ Middle ☐ Youngest ☐ Twin

Parent Name:		**Parent Name:**	
Parent Occupation:		**Parent Occupation:**	
Number of Siblings:			
Sibling Names:			

PERSONALITY

Personality Type: ☐ Introvert ☐ Extrovert

Demeanor/Temperament:
☐ Friendly ☐ Cheerful ☐ Arrogant/Haughty ☐ Reserved
☐ Down to Earth ☐ Stoic ☐ Self-Absorbed ☐ Brooding
☐ Laidback ☐ Uptight ☐ Excitable ☐ Surly

Character Trait: ☐ Hero ☐ Antihero ☐ Villain
☐ Martyr ☐ Victim

Communication Style: ☐ Nonverbal ☐ Monosyllabic ☐ Normal
☐ Speaks only when spoken to ☐ Gregarious ☐ Sign Language

Phobias:

Quirks:

Unhealthy Habits: ☐ Tobacco ☐ Alcohol ☐ Drugs

Strengths/Weaknesses:

Closely Held Secret:

SEXUALITY

Sexual Partner Preference: ☐ Heterosexual ☐ Homosexual
☐ Bisexual ☐ Asexual ☐ Other:

Sexual Experience:
☐ Virgin ☐ Novice ☐ Experienced

Type of Sex Preferred:
☐ Vanilla/Traditional ☐ BDSM ☐ Kink ☐ Multiples ☐ Swing
☐ Other:

FASHION STYLE

Personal Preference: ☐ Professional ☐ Business Casual ☐ Casual
☐ Athletic Wear ☐ Glam ☐ Minimalist ☐ Edgy

Fit: ☐ Tailored ☐ Figure-Hugging ☐ Skin Tight
☐ Loose ☐ Baggy ☐ Skimpy

RELATIONSHIPS

Family Structure: ☐ Close Knit ☐ Estranged ☐ Absent ☐ Unknown

Favorite Relative:

Closest Friend:

Work Buddy/Spouse:

As a Neighbor: ☐ Reclusive ☐ Friendly (knows their names)
☐ Knows by Sight Only ☐ No neighbors

Protagonist # 10

First Name:		Last Name:	
Name Meaning:		Name Meaning:	
Birth Month:		Age:	

Sexual Identity: ☐ Male ☐ Female ☐ Transgender ☐ Nonbinary

Race: ☐ White ☐ Black ☐ Native American ☐ Asian
☐ Pacific Islander ☐ Hispanic ☐ Mixed Race

Ethnicity/ Ancestry:		Religion:	

Species: ☐ Human ☐ Alien ☐ Vampire ☐ Shifter ☐ Fae
☐ Ghost ☐ Mythological god ☐ Witch/Mage ☐ Demon
☐ Mermaid ☐ Djinn ☐ Angels ☐ Gargoyles ☐ Cyborg

Education: ☐ PhD ☐ Masters ☐ 4-year ☐ 2-year ☐ Technical School
☐ High School Graduate ☐ GED ☐ HS Drop Out

Languages: ☐ English ☐ Mandarin ☐ Hindi ☐ Spanish
☐ French ☐ Arabic ☐ Russian ☐ ASL

Dialect/Accent:

Marital Status: ☐ Single ☐ Married ☐ Widowed
☐ Divorced ☐ Separated ☐ Polygamist

Skills/ Hobbies:		Pets:	

Socioeconomic Status: ☐ Top 2% ☐ Wealthy ☐ Poor
☐ Upper Middle Class ☐ Middle Class ☐ Lower Class

Occupation		Employer	

Military: ☐ Never Served ☐ Active Duty ☐ Retired
☐ Honorable Discharge ☐ Dishonorable Discharge

Branch Served:		Years Served:	

Rank/Title:

Criminal Record: ☐ None ☐ Misdemeanor ☐ Felony

DESCRIPTION

Height:		**Weight:**	
Eye Color:		**Hair Color:**	

Complexion / Skin Tone:

Hair Texture:		**Hair Length:**	

Shape of Face: ☐ Square ☐ Oval ☐ Rectangle/Oblong ☐ Round
☐ Diamond ☐ Triangle

Distinguishing Marks:		**Tattoos:**	

Vision: ☐ 20/20   ☐ Glasses   ☐ Contacts   ☐ Blind
☐ Astigmatism   ☐ Nearsighted   ☐ Farsighted   ☐ Cataracts

Physical Limitations:		**Mental Limitations:**	
Medical Conditions:		**Allergies:**	

Body Type: ☐ Ectomorph   ☐ Mesomorph   ☐ Endomorph

Body Shape (female):   ☐ Rectangle/Straight   ☐ Apple
☐ Pear/Triangle   ☐ Hourglass

Bust Size: ☐ AA ☐ A ☐ B ☐ C ☐ D ☐ DD ☐ E ☐ F ☐ G ☐ Larger

BACKGROUND

Native Country:		**Native Language:**	
State/ Provence:		**City / Town:**	

Childhood Home: ☐ Single Family ☐ Townhome ☐ Apartment/Condo
☐ Mobile Home ☐ Farm ☐ Ranch
☐ Multiple Residences/Homes ☐ Homeless

Raised by: ☐ Both Parents ☐ Single Parent ☐ Relative
☐ Foster Care ☐ Orphan ☐ Adopted ☐ Non-Relative

Birth Order: ☐ Oldest ☐ Middle ☐ Youngest ☐ Twin

Parent Name:		**Parent Name:**	
Parent Occupation:		**Parent Occupation:**	

Number of Siblings:

Sibling Names:

PERSONALITY

Personality Type: ☐ Introvert ☐ Extrovert

Demeanor/Temperament:
☐ Friendly ☐ Cheerful ☐ Arrogant/Haughty ☐ Reserved
☐ Down to Earth ☐ Stoic ☐ Self-Absorbed ☐ Brooding
☐ Laidback ☐ Uptight ☐ Excitable ☐ Surly

Character Trait: ☐ Hero ☐ Antihero ☐ Villain
☐ Martyr ☐ Victim

Communication Style: ☐ Nonverbal ☐ Monosyllabic ☐ Normal
☐ Speaks only when spoken to ☐ Gregarious ☐ Sign Language

Phobias:

Quirks:

Unhealthy Habits: ☐ Tobacco ☐ Alcohol ☐ Drugs

Strengths/Weaknesses:

Closely Held Secret:

SEXUALITY

Sexual Partner Preference: ☐ Heterosexual ☐ Homosexual
☐ Bisexual ☐ Asexual ☐ Other:

Sexual Experience:
☐ Virgin ☐ Novice ☐ Experienced

Type of Sex Preferred:
☐ Vanilla/Traditional ☐ BDSM ☐ Kink ☐ Multiples ☐ Swing
☐ Other:

FASHION STYLE

Personal Preference: ☐ Professional ☐ Business Casual ☐ Casual
☐ Athletic Wear ☐ Glam ☐ Minimalist ☐ Edgy

Fit: ☐ Tailored ☐ Figure-Hugging ☐ Skin Tight
☐ Loose ☐ Baggy ☐ Skimpy

RELATIONSHIPS

Family Structure: ☐ Close Knit ☐ Estranged ☐ Absent ☐ Unknown

Favorite Relative:

Closest Friend:

Work Buddy/Spouse:

As a Neighbor: ☐ Reclusive ☐ Friendly (knows their names)
☐ Knows by Sight Only ☐ No neighbors

Notes, Research, Links

Notes, Research, Links

Notes, Research, Links

Notes, Research, Links